CREATING YOUR HEAVEN ON EARTH

Meagan M. O'Nan

# CREATING YOUR HEAVEN ON EARTH

*Unveiling the Truth
that Was Always There*

Dreamriver Press

Dreamriver Press LLC
www.dreamriverpress.com
or contact at:
12 Franklin Avenue
Flourtown, PA 19031-2006
U.S.A.

First Dreamriver Press edition, 2008

ISBN-13:  978-0-9797908-1-2
ISBN-10:  0-9797908-1-6

Library of Congress Control Number:  2008929284


Designed by George D. Matthiopoulos


Printed and bound in The United States of America

Through the process of creating this piece, I have learned the value of Love as it is equated with God. I am blown away by the action and not just the knowing. I am grateful to those in my life who have taught me and challenged me to let go and discover the true meaning of Real Love ... it is the reason we are here and the inspiration behind our Truth.

*The moment speaks clearly of who I am, and every moment is meant to be as beautiful as the next ... if it is given the attention it deserves. To see the soul of another is to see the soul of myself. Life ... how we make it so complicated in a world in which society always seems to win. The struggle is always this ... lack of letting go, which hinders the acceptance of the divine in our own heart. My divine is yours as well. Love is an abiding, never-ending circle. Loving yourself means you simply love others.*

Meagan M. O'Nan holds two Master's degrees in the field of disability and is completing her certification as a Spiritual Life Coach. She believes that all people have a Divine nature and that everyone is capable of achieving their soul's dreams. She lives in Fort Collins, Colorado, and enjoys the inspiring scenery and sunshine that Colorado has to offer. Meagan's dream is to motivate others to discover what is true for them. For more information, please visit www.meaganonan.com

# TABLE OF CONTENTS

CONTENTS

# FOREWORD

Words encapsulate and transmit energy. Once in a while a word or phrase zings us, communicating truth that permeates the thick armor of our consciousness that most of us build to protect ourselves from the bombardment of over-stimulation. Meagan's words and phrases in this book hold many truth-zinging words and phrases—such as:

> … heaven begins inside us …
> the moment represents living in love …
> in the moment we are free …

Take time to savor the precious gems contained here. They house the potential to shore up the foundation of your life, thoughts, beliefs, emotions and patterns of behavior to support the essential you.

I acknowledge the open vulnerability with which Meagan describes her experiences, her eye-opening short stories and exercises to assist you in touching the beauty within. I think you will find them extremely valuable, as I did. They provide many different facets to guide us to the singular truth of who we really are and that we are one.

This is a book to read when you are in need of inspiration, feel downtrodden, fearful, doubt the truth of who you are or when you simply want to bask in the beauty of love. The saliency of choice shines through Meagan's words and points the way to truth.

Stripping away the observable, *Creating Your Heaven on Earth* reveals the underlying, unseen reality of Being. Bask in the stark and glorious simplicity of unseen reality.

While you may have encountered the concepts presented in *Creating Your Heaven on Earth*, the poignancy that Meagan's words carry melts your heart, and invites you to walk along the journey leading to self-discovery.

Read these pages and glimpse heaven—better yet, create heaven.

*Joan C. King*
June 2, 2008

# INTRODUCTION

Life on earth is an opportunity for us to discover our own personal truth in order to create a place that we can call OUR heaven. Is joy not what we want and desire right now and forever? What would life be like without joy? I do not claim that there is one perfect way to find this joy, the truth, our purpose or to defining who we are. All I know is that we are all perfect... complete and holy expressions of the Divine. There are many paths to joy, truth, and purpose, and there are many ways to define God, Love, or a Higher Power. Right and wrong are defined by the person observing his or her own world. With these considerations in mind, this book is an expression of my spirit, my purpose, and I share it with those whose hands it falls into. It reflects nothing less and nothing more than a part of my truth. Naturally, I have been influenced by the stories of other people and these have assisted in my spiritual development. I share what is true for me as merely an offer of what I believe—that heaven begins inside us. I hope that perhaps this will resonate in your own heart... and that you will find greater peace and joy in your life. I am proud to be walking this fulfilling journey with each of you.

Who are usually the first ones to get on the dance floor at a wedding reception? The children are. In all of their glory, maintaining their carefree spirit, their true souls shine...and we are attracted to their freedom to just dance, so we watch. With no worries, no fears, the children smile, waving their arms and twirling...showing us that we too have the freedom to create our heaven on earth. The children look like spirits floating...separate souls sending the energy of love our way. The innocence of children dancing is pure...just as is their spirit...just as are our spirits. Wouldn't it be nice to dance again and not care? Wouldn't it be nice to be fully aware in every moment, appreciating the freedom to be exactly who we are meant to be?

Through our divine selves we can find our innocence and create our heaven on this earth. There is no reason why we should wait until our physical selves disappear before we live within and experience the bliss that is right before our very eyes. Now is the moment to open our spirits, discover our true selves...our divine souls, so that our lives become connected to joy and happiness. This is a dream worth living, and guess what...you are in charge of your destiny, so you can make it happen! The energy and the beauty of your God, your Higher Power, your Divine Self, is right inside you waiting for a chance to explore the depths of the moment.

Walk through heaven with me ... and find that your worries, your fears, and your doubts are but thoughts that can be forgotten. Imagine being in a place of bliss, where life is carefree and joyous ... that place can be here on earth.

Be aware that throughout the book you will find a progression with the concepts being explained as you read on. The intention is to answer your questions as you move forward through the chapters.

## CHAPTER 1

### What is God? Energy ... Love ... One and the Same

*All of our experiences, whether ours or anothers, affect who we are and lead us not only to ask the questions of life, but to find the answers as well.*

Who is God to you? Who is this Energy, this Being, this Infinite Power? Whether God is a She or a He, an energy, a tangible or intangible presence, that which created the earth or that which did not ... God is still who or what we create it to be. Omnipotent in Its essence, this Love is to be discovered by us all if we open our hearts to the possibility that truth is within us. God is Love ... and Love is God. There is no correct or incorrect way to name God, so name It in a way that is comfortable for you.

In a world that often defines itself by messages of war, violence, hunger, disease, imperfection, and poverty, it is easy to misinterpret our own peace, the interpretation of which can play an important part in changing the world around us. If we were all at peace and had joy in our hearts, then imagine the heaven that would result. What does it look like to you? Why must we wait until our physical state has ended to experience bliss? We are all worthy and capable of joy, peace, clarity and, YES, heaven on earth now.

Whether you believe in heaven, hell, reincarnation, or nothing at all, you are still here at this very moment, reading this very page ... which presumably means that you are looking to enhance your own happiness. We are all worthy of experiencing happiness, a happiness that begins inside us. This is a journey that has meaning, that has purpose, and to discover that purpose is to find the greatest truth—that heaven does, in fact, exist on earth.

When you have found the divine part of your heart, you have found God ... you have found Love; thus, you have begun to experience the qualities of the earth-existence that we so often neglect. You can be like the children at those wedding receptions, who express the presence of a spirit, floating and recognizing the beauty of our world through gratitude.

Understand that you cannot neglect yourself. You must love your own unique beauty, and then the discovery of your gifts will help you shine. When you shine, your spirit is allowing itself to be shown, and you find that the more you love yourself, the more you love others.

Peace and harmony are right before us: will we choose to shine, or will we neglect our truth ... our own heart? If we live in truth, then we create truth ... and the truth can only be created by us. Once we allow our truth to be revealed, it creates a ripple effect on those around us, and it transforms our world, because it is a world that we have constructed ourselves. While living in accordance with our truth, we continuously find ourselves in service to a world that needs our love. Our love is magnified by the discovery of our Divine Self and by the actions which we partake in once we have made our discovery. If we solely choose to follow our truth then it is clear that others will resonate with our love and will be affected by the depth of unconditional love. When we start to live according to and expressing our own personal truth, we may often find that others start living according to their truths as well.

No matter what your background is, no matter what your story is, no matter where you want to go or where you want to end up ... it is okay to be yourself. You do not have to be what anyone wants you to be ... you only have to be you. By seizing the opportunity to take any moment to discover your truth, you will come to realize that your awareness of time is starting to disappear. When you begin to live in your truth, then looking at your watch becomes an action that you partake in less and less. Has there ever been a moment when you enjoyed what you were doing so much that you forgot what time it was? This is what I mean when I say your awareness of time is starting to disappear; when we live in our truth, then we enjoy each moment, and time becomes less and less important.

And so, this God, this Being, in whichever way we conceive It, dwells within us, pushing us gracefully through a life that is truly meant to be beautiful. You may ask why, if life is meant to be beautiful, is your life so confusing and hard all the time? My answer to you is ... keep reading.

Let's now take a look at what the great teachers through history have said about God. There have been many great teachers. Buddha, Mohammad, and Jesus linger in many of our minds as people who understood the truth of life. The one with whom I am most familiar is Jesus. Growing up, I heard many stories of this man's life on earth, and his teachings always intrigued me. I have always felt connected to this man, and eventually I realized by reading about him, that we are all (big and small, past or present) a part of one another ... we are all a piece of the same Being, a part of the same creation.

Jesus', Buddha's, and Mohammad's lives all had meaning through their expression of unconditional love. Usually, we hear about Jesus' physical death, and in my society we mourn his death. Both in his own time and during subsequent history, Jesus has not been understood by some, and those that have seemed to understand him have usually remained silent because no words could express the meaning of complete and unconditional love. The life of Jesus is one to pay attention to. He was so simple in his essence, his words so eloquent, and his message so vibrant. "Whoever receives you, receives me, and whoever receives me receives the one who sent me" (Matt. 10:40). In this single statement, it is my perception that Jesus is making a reference to us as the human race. Saying that, we are all truly ONE and the same. Jesus is saying, I am connected to you and you are connected to me, and we are all a part of God.

It is my belief that there is one powerful approach that enables us to appreciate and experience a sense of our oneness, and that is *living in the moment.* This comprised another important part of this man's teachings as revealed through sayings such as, "Do not worry about tomorrow; tomorrow will take care of itself" (Matt. 6:34). Another great teacher, Buddha, once said, "Do not dwell in the past, do not dream of the future, concentrate the mind on the present moment." Two great teachers, two great men, along with many more throughout history, saying exactly the same thing—the moment to live is now, the moment to love is now, the moment to breathe is NOW. By living in the moment, these two men discovered peace, they discovered purpose ... and their words continue to move.

Through this we can see that Buddha, Jesus and, indeed, Mohammad, founder of Islam and the Muslim faith, all taught that, if we live in the moment, then we learn to love who we are and our true wealth is able to shine outward. By living in the moment, we find that people often "do good" for the world, because the moment represents living in love. Mohammad once stated, "A man's true wealth is the good he does in the world." And I believe that this "true wealth" comes from living in the moment and a trust in our own soul. Ernest Holmes, founder of Religious Science, once said, "And more than everything else, we believe in our own soul; the only immediate testimony you and I will ever have, that we exist, or that God exists, or that Jesus (or Mohammad or Buddha) showed us a way." So, the truth is spiraled by many different voices, many teachers, many different ways of thinking and approaching this life; ultimately, the truth is simply found within each of us.

We look at the lives of those who seem to be fulfilled and wise without recognizing how we can also be fulfilled. We are constantly looking for the outside world to provide the answers, and yet, we always come back to the same question: what is next? It is the moment to start to believe that your fulfillment and your purpose is just as wonderful and just as meaningful as Mohammad's, Jesus', Ernest Holmes' and Buddha's. How is it that you can find this fulfillment? "Ask and it will be given to you; seek and you will find; knock and the door will be opened to you" (Matt. 7:7). Now that we have reflected on the beliefs of some of the great teachers throughout history, let's start the "asking, seeking and knocking at the door" by considering what the meaning of Spirit, God or Love is to each of us.

At some point in each of our lives we question the existence of God and of creation because we see all that is going wrong in the world. We may ask why, if God is love, do certain things happen? My answer is this ... free will. As I have chosen my path, so has every other being that has ever lived, or that is alive. One purpose in which we serve as human beings is to express and receive love; however, not every individual has chosen the path of peace and joy. What about those who are born into situations of injustice or unfairness? Well, no situation is too great to see the beauty of what is before us. Love is everywhere; life is happening... what will you choose to make of it? This may be a bold question, but really, what do you truly want out of this life? Peace, joy, happiness, patience? Anger, sadness, unhappiness? An important point to make at this juncture is that all emotions are aspects of Divine Love. I believe that in the Divine itself there is no negative or positive... there is no dualism at all; negative and positive are measures we have created (for comparison purposes) in our (mistaken) belief that we need to define where we stand with ourselves and with others. The important question to ask yourself is, what emotions work for you to evoke your truth?

Have you ever heard of Viktor Frankl? Frankl earned his M.D. in neurology and psychiatry and his Ph.D. in philosophy from the University of Vienna. During World War II he was sent to Theresienstadt and then to Auschwitz and other concentration camps. Frankl chose to see life as a choice in personal perspective and attitude and wrote many books on the individual and very personal nature of the meaning of someone's life. Having lived through four Nazi death camps, Frankl offers the thought that all of life has meaning that can never be taken away from the individual. Only the individual can by their own choice disregard their purpose and meaning. Viktor Frankl is a great example of a person who chose to see the world as something magnificent in the midst of one of the most horrific events in our known history. Frankl was able to survive because he believed in his purpose and taught that every person's life on earth has a meaning, or a purpose, that is expressed as Divine creativity. Frankl's teachings show us that our spirits are truly a part of the Divine, and if we choose to come in contact with that part of ourselves, we can have joy; we can have peace; and we can have fulfillment.

The essence of spirit, of fulfillment (that which Frankl talks about), of God, has no physical nature. Although we are focused on issues of time, how we look, or what people may think, our usual perceptions of what is around us on this earth are not the reality. Reality and indeed heaven are to be experienced in the moment. If we focus our attention on the present moment (right NOW) then we cannot miss the spirit surrounding us. You can call it God, Love, Energy, or a Higher Being ... regardless, the truth does not change. In the moment we are free of judgment, of questions, of confusion, and it is abundant in joy, peace, and fulfillment. I will continue to explain this concept later.

For now, take a moment to look around you … the trees, the flowers, the ocean, the mountains, any animals of the household, a person you love … anything and everything serves as a source of Energy, a source of God. The sooner we recognize this truth, the sooner we can gain a sense of freedom through the clarity it gives. God, Love, Creator and Energy exist because you exist … as it is. Let it be.

The world tells us that we have to be perfect in every way, and perfection and imperfection can be defined in so many different ways. Discovering who we are helps us to discover what God is and vice versa. Society tells us that we have to be skinny, we have to get married, we have to be a particular religion, we have to be successful, we have to be heterosexual, etc. At some point we realize everything we are not and never give ourselves an opportunity to see all that we are. Someone once told me that it is your ability, not your disability, that matters. There is truth in that, because if we are trying to live up to what everyone else wants us to be, then we find that we are "disabled" in some manner. The term disability is often a figure of speech used to label people who have an impairment that may limit their ability to perform daily activities (such as walking, seeing, etc.). Some people even consider people with disabilities to be "abnormal." However, we all have abilities and disabilities, so in a sense we are all abnormal. This abnormality or uniqueness is something to be appreciated in ourselves and in others. Are you normal? I'm not.

So, really, why do we continue to expect so much out of ourselves when we know that we can never attain worldly perfection? The idea that we can or even should achieve worldly perfection is a lie, it is a false goal that can only lead an individual to begin to crush the very nature of their own beauty. We are all "imperfect" in a worldly sense. The sooner that society's requests are deleted from our expectations, the quicker we will find the perfection that is already within us. Living in the moment, and acknowledging the presence of unconditional love is the key to the end of flaws and not feeling good enough.

Changing our perspective on how we view ourselves is an inward search that cannot end in disappointment. Instead of saying, "I'll never be good enough," say "I am good enough," because, guess what ... you are good enough, and I am good enough! When you find your own personal truth then you see that you are perfect, because your truth is perfect. If you are living in the moment then you recognize your truth. If you recognize your truth, then you have discovered your spirit (the essence of God). If you have found your spirit, then you begin to see the spirit of others with no pre-judgment. And if you can view the world through the moment without a tainted perspective ... then, trust me, you have discovered heaven, your heaven ... your perfection.

# CHAPTER 2

## The Past, the Present, the Future

*We do not grow absolutely, chronologically. We grow sometimes in one dimension, and not in another; unevenly. We grow partially. We are relative. We are mature in one realm, childish in another. The past, present, and future mingle and pull us backward, forward, or fix us in the present. We are made up of layers, cells, constellations.*

Anais Nin

L anguage teaches us the importance of the past, the present, and the future through our using different tenses when speaking. We learn early in life that if we misbehave as a child we will later be punished. We are taught to fear outcomes because our behavior might not have been fitting for how we should have behaved. So, we are punished, told to never do it again, and we don't quite understand why the behavior was incorrect, only that it was bad. This same lesson is one that resonates into adulthood. Somehow, we grow up learning to hesitate in our actions because we fear the outcome. For instance, I have always wanted to be a writer, but instead I went to college three times to get an undergraduate and two graduate degrees that are not related to writing. This has all been a part of my self-realization process; however, there has been a doubt embedded in me, fearing the outcome of possible failure. Yes, POSSIBLE failure.

It is often simple to allow ourselves to stay comfortable in our current state…fearing, and never letting go of the past or the future. However, the truth of the matter is the past is over and the future is not here yet. So, what's important? Right now. The gift of discovering the present moment is one that we have all experienced, but it is the letting go of what is already done and what has not yet happened that is the challenge. However, through letting go, we experience a freedom of joy.

Letting go of the past and the future can seem like a very daunting task to some. We often allow the past and the future to be a hindrance to the right now. How can we achieve anything in a particular moment if what once happened or what might happen is claiming our attention?

When we experience pain in our lives, the next time a similar situation occurs we hesitate due to a lack of trust caused by our previous encounter. Similarly, when we are worried about an outcome and our worries come alive, then we are setting ourselves up for failure by becoming conditioned to pay too much attention to something that might or might not happen in the future. With this in mind, try to establish a connection with your fears and note if they are actually a part of the past or an illusion of the future. I have always said that it is better to accept our vulnerability than to never experience what the moment will bring.

Many people consider that the past defines who we are. On the contrary, it doesn't define who we are; it simply brings us to where we are on our path. And, guess what … that is not a bad thing. I am in no way attempting to answer all of life's questions. I am only claiming what has been true for me. I know that what I have learned has been most powerful when I have allowed the past to be what it is (just something in your mind), not what it was (an actual, possibly painful, experience). I can change nothing that has already occurred, but I have every opportunity to claim what is in front of me … by fully accepting and experiencing the moment, the acceptance of right now. To take a breath of acceptance is

29

to take a breath of freedom. The cleansing of the heart is felt within the entire body as we learn continually to let go, to continue to allow the process of life to take place as it is, to breathe deeply.

I once read that the secret of life is "not minding what happens." We are taught that it is important to take control in order to make sure that things happen as we wish. But, with this way of thinking, we continually find ourselves struggling to understand why situations do not in fact correspond to what we are wanting. As a child, I remember hearing the words "have faith." To me, the meaning of *to have faith* is not with a religious connotation. It simply means to believe, to trust, but whatever you choose to call that which you trust in is up to you. For me, I trust in the process that we are so freely offered, the process of having an option of whether to trust or not that the Divine layout of our world is one that creates itself; a trust based on our belief that we can manifest all that is in alignment with our truth.

Basically, I am finding that when I choose to let go of what *was* or what *might be* and am open to not minding what happens, then all that I truly want in the depth of my heart (the place where I consider my Light to be—call it God, Higher Power or whatever) will be laid before me at the appropriate time.

Abundance of joy, peace, happiness is a matter of perception; a matter of deciphering the difference between accepting what society tells us (that we are not good enough) and pushing unhelpful thoughts aside and accepting that all is well...in this moment. I add this simply because this moment is all that we truly have.

The wholeness in which we all have a part to play is already whole. There is nothing to search for. Your truth is right inside your heart...waiting for its true expression. When our truth is given the permission to come forth, then we will find that faith is the key to the next step that we will take. The secret to life is not minding what happens—this means, if you really want a hamburger from your chosen place to eat, and they are out of beef, then either get a turkey burger or leave. No one ever said you had to stay and complain. Not minding what happens involves accepting that all is perfect just as it is.

I once knew a woman who was in constant fear of what might happen. Due to her past she feared outcomes. She was living a lonely life, constantly searching for peace, but never willing to let go of what had once happened many years before. She had closed her heart to a world that wanted to love her, and she had sunk through her bitterness and was left trying to figure a way out of her depression. She wasn't able to step outside of the influence of the past or the future. The important point here is that this woman had made a choice to continue to experience sadness. Joy was an option ... joy is always a choice ... and yes, anyone can have it. I do still know this woman very well, and when I saw her last she had a smile on her face. This smile struck me, and I asked her why she was so happy. She replied, "I have finally discovered the moment." The truth that she had discovered was powerful and meaningful for her, and if the moment is all that she needed to find, then there is no more truth than that to find.

If our attention is given to the past and future and our lives revolve around unrealistic expectations, deadlines and fears, the result is sure to be self-disapproval. Now is the moment to stop being the victim and to claim victory through the joy that comes through awareness of what is in front of us. Remember, no one can give us peace but ourselves.

Let's take a look at what it actually means to *live in the moment*. Have you ever looked at a newborn baby in awe of its innocence and grace? Have you ever watched the vastness of the ocean and understood the concept of eternity? Have you ever felt so much love for another person that you felt as though your heart would burst? All of these separate experiences have the same cause ... they result from living in the moment.

I simply cannot pass judgment (I am using judgment as only a figure of speech) on a newborn child because it has not yet experienced life in the way I see it. As a result, when I approach a newborn child I approach it as it is ... innocent and pure. This kind of interaction is one of Love ... and only in the moment can Love/God be fully experienced ... in the moment there are no other thoughts ... only the thought for the child that is before us. What if we approached all people in this way? To approach all people as though they each are a child of Love is to move toward the realization of what is Divine perfection. Living in the moment is an expression of Love, of Energy, of God.

If you have ever stared at an ocean, then you have probably been in awe of its depth and how it seems to go on and on. The magnitude of such an incredible sight is one that clarifies the concept of eternity. If I am staring at the ocean in awe and I feel a peace within because of its astounding beauty, then again I have found the moment. Anytime that love is carried into your heart, notice that the past and the future do not exist in that moment. The ocean and the newborn child represent a part of God, a part of Love, a realization that comes through acknowledging the moment. And if you are able to be present in the moment then you will never cease to be comfortable in your eternal nature.

Finally, if you have ever loved someone you will know the amount to which true love can affect you. You may have noticed that when a person you love walks into a room your heart beats faster. Through that feeling—the feeling you get when your loved one touches you, speaks to you, laughs with you, or tells you that they love you—you have discovered the power of love by choosing to live in the now. The cycle is the same no matter what moment you choose fully to be a part of. I am sitting at a desk right now with a soft drink, scribbled outlines, and a sketch from an artist in front of me. You might say, "How exciting is that?" Well, I look at all three objects as they are one and the same through being experienced in this moment … they are objects that have been crafted by different hands and, therefore, connect me to others. Through this I only find love. Only in the moment are Love, God and Eternity freely expressed and experienced.

You get to choose what you would like to be a part of … the past, the present, or the future. I will show you how to determine the differences between what is evident when you can focus your attention on the right now - the truth, and what is false. Just remember one thing—this life is your choice and only you can change the way you see your heaven.

# CHAPTER 3

## This God, this Being ... Is Found in the Moment

*Life can be found only in the present moment. The past is gone,
the future is not yet here, and if we do not go back to ourselves
in the present moment, we cannot be in touch with life.*

Thich Nhat Hanh

We all view our God, Higher Power, or Being in various ways. Some may say that this Being is evident through prayer; that It is found in stillness; that there are many Gods; that God answers our questions; or that God does not even exist. One way or another God is what we create It to be, even if we make It not exist. Let me tell you what further conclusions I have drawn on this issue, simply because they appear to be working for me. Whatever it is that you believe, It is somehow connected to the essence of life and the essence of our purpose ... which is to love and be loved. There is no greater emotion or feeling than this. If love is the bliss of life, then surely my God and your Higher Power, or my Higher Power and your God are actually the core of our existence; they are love. If there is no God then what is there to argue about? And if there is a God, and if God is love, isn't it fair to say that we all see this Being in a similar way?

In a world of total togetherness we would find no need to appreciate joy, love, or peace because we could not know anything different; therefore, there is no need for the quest for God, Creativity, Love, or Energy to exist in our everyday lives. It is the challenges of life that often bring us back to the direct experience of God or Love, and that is what keeps us moving. The experience of this Love is what gives us the extra push to continue defining the moment when Love (or God) expresses itself ... and that is what keeps us moving. Love is the part of us that gives us the extra push to continue. Wouldn't it be nice to experience love at all times? That would be heaven.

So, the question is not what you believe or how you believe it ... it is, can you see or experience the beauty of every moment? Every second that passes is an opportunity to open your eyes to the details that are before you.

Living in the moment helps you to see that everything is black and white. Black and white? Are there not other colors in the universe? When I use the terms black and white here they are a metaphor for the choice you have regarding whether to live in love or not to. By this I mean that when we see what is really going on, we see that everything is really quite simple (black and white) and that we no longer need to confuse ourselves with the grey areas. Life is clearly how we view it to be. As a person who has discovered the realm of beauty in day-to-day life, and as a person who has also experienced NOT acknowledging this beauty, I am finding that the essence of what governs my perception is whether I am aware of love ... or not. You can call this what you want ... Love, God, a Higher Power ... but, ultimately this essence is simply what it is perceived to be as it settles in your own heart —what seems true for you.

As a believer that we are incarnations of the Divine ... yes, all of us ... I find that we have the choice to see our own divinity or not. When we find that we are a physical being expressing our eternal spirit and we can look and listen to what stillness is telling us, then we create the opportunity to see that the "grey" areas of life are simply a misperception, a judgment, a destructive thought, a misinterpreted desire, or a result of having learned something incorrectly. In general we can say that something has happened that we have allowed to make us focus on our earthly imperfections. Either we think we are perfect, divine beings, or we think we are not. Our thoughts are what control our outcomes—the grey areas—and our hearts give us the clear answers regarding the truth of the situation.

In a physical world that attempts to mold us into thinking that we are never enough, the spiritual realm of life is available to assist in the recognition of what truly is. If we are able to step outside ourselves, then we find that our bodies are the paintbrush and our spirits the canvas on which we create our lives. Either you choose to live in love ... or you choose to not live in love. Whenever you question a decision or struggle to choose which path you are to take, then you are contemplating that which is not y*our* truth—a fear, a worry, or a result that has not yet happened. Life is exactly what we make it.

I believe that we have the power to see our beauty. The beauty of the world was so evident as a child, so what got in the way? The answer: the grey areas got in the way ... how we were told to live, what we were told to believe, what we were told to think is right, but isn't right for us, etc. This is part of the human condition; however, we each have the ability to come from and come into conciousness. My ego is the result of what I wish to control, of what I wish to fulfill, a fulfillment that is not of Truth, of God, of Love. Pushing the ego aside enables us to put things in clear perspective and see them for what they truly are. Listening to what our hearts are telling us is equivalent to listening to what Love, what God, what our Higher Power is showing us as part of our truth, our journey, our purpose, our passion! I want to live as an individual who loves who she is so that she can love others on a greater level; I want to be a spirit that can sit in silence and radiate light; I want to be a person that is willing to work on weeding out the grey areas so that the black and white become clearer and clearer. I already am that person, and you already are that person if you choose to be.

For me, it is helpful to know that however I was created— whether I have lived other lives or if I will live more lives to come—I was created from Love ... and that it is the purpose of my existence, to expand that which was and is the meaning of living ... Love. All of the great spiritual leaders of the world may approach the philosophy and spirituality of life in different ways, but the core concept that is always apparent is the knowing that we are each an expression of LOVE, that we have free will, and that we can thus choose to express this Love further by loving one another. We search and search for another person to fulfill our desires, but it is not another that will fulfill you … it is you that will fulfill yourself. You are already full … you just might not feel it yet.

So, in walking this earth, floating as a being who has meaning and a purpose, there is an opportunity to choose between "YES, I will live in love." and "NO, I will not live in love." If happiness, joy, and peace are to dwell within, then take the opportunity to just listen to what is already within you—that which was there when you were a child; that which is only of Love. You are perfect the way you are … that is the message.

Fully experiencing "the moment" or "the now" helps to produce an appreciation for life. The moment is when you notice the trees, the flowers, the laugh of another, the cool breeze on a hot day, the sight of a sunset, the voice of someone you love, the excitement of your puppy when you return home from a day at work, or the many instances when there are no worries, no fears, no deadlines. *Now* is right now as you read this book. It is difficult to describe what it means to be fully aware in the moment because in the now love is fully expressed and experienced. Can you fully comprehend the concepts of Love, Eternity, or God? Then surely what we experience when living in *the moment* cannot be clearly described … that is why all of these concepts are so tough to grasp.

As human beings we crave touch, the tangible essence of life—a part that we know exists because we can feel it. Love, God, peace or faith cannot be touched with your hand nor seen with your eyes. It is all simply a belief that something besides ourselves is out there showing us that we are a part of something absolutely fascinating. This thing called life is not a challenge, but an opportunity to show our light by being who we know we are and believing that each moment is ours to claim.

Notice your breath as you read. Take a few moments from reading and breathe in through your nose and out through your mouth ... inhale, exhale, over and over. There is nothing but your breath ... just listen and focus on you and your breath for five minutes.

Guess what? You have just experienced a glimpse of *the now*! When I first realized the glory of every second, I wanted it more and more. So I would focus on my breathing to put me in the moment and I was easily addicted. Once I decided to focus on my breath then the details of the world became so vibrant. It was as though I could have an overwhelming feeling of love any time I wanted it. Was this some major discovery that took years of practice and a lot of studying? Absolutely not. When I was a college student, I happened to notice that when I let go of the past and the future and discovered *the moment*, then bits and pieces of my purpose became clearer and clearer. And as your purpose unfolds then your heaven starts to become a reality. The experience of *living in the moment* can ultimately be described as living in beauty, in Love, as one of the world's perfect creations. How can any creation of God, of Love, of Energy be less than perfect?

It soon became clear to me that what you experience through focusing on *the moment* changes your perspective. Since I was little, I have always loved animals. I have always felt a strange connection to them as if we were communicating in a silent language called *the moment*. I have always felt like my pets or someone else's pets could see right through me and were able to feed of my energy. Although there is no simple explanation for the way we feel about our pets, other than love, I opt to say that perhaps our pets understand what *the moment* is. Someone once told me that *dog* is *god* spelled backwards. It was at that moment that I realized why I have always been so enamored with the love my dogs seem unconditionally and trustingly to give to me. Without a thought crossing their minds, my dogs love me all the time in every moment, therefore displaying the most important part of our existence ... living in *the moment*. Again, it is this ability to live in *the moment* that allows for *conditions* to disappear and the *unconditional* expression of love to become evident. Here is a story I once heard:

> A veterinarian had been called to examine a ten-year-old Irish wolfhound named Belker. The dog's owners, Ron, his wife, Lisa, and their little boy, Shane, were all very attached to Belker, and they were hoping for a miracle. She examined Belker and found he was dying of cancer. She told the family that she couldn't do anything for Belker, and offered to perform the euthanasia procedure for the old dog in their home. As she made arrangements, Ron and Lisa told her that they thought it would be good for six-year-old Shane to observe the procedure. They felt as though Shane might learn something from the experience.
>
> The next day, the veterinarian felt the familiar catch in her throat as Belker's family surrounded her. Shane seemed so calm, petting the old dog for the last time, that she wondered if he understood what was going on. Within a few minutes, Belker slipped peacefully away. The little boy seemed to accept Belker's transition without any difficulty or confusion. They all sat together for a while after Belker's death, wondering aloud about the sad fact that animal lives are shorter than human lives. Shane, who had been listening quietly, piped up, "I know why." Startled, they all turned to him. What came out of his mouth next stunned the veterinarian. She'd never heard a more comforting explanation.
>
> He said, "People are born so that they can learn how to

live a good life—like loving everybody all the time and being nice, right?" The six-year-old continued, "Well, dogs already know how to do that, so they don't have to stay as long."

Our pets are an example to us ... we are not the example to them. We try to teach them tricks, make them sit or stop their annoying barking, but really, they are the ones who have us "chasing our own tails." Somehow they secretly show us that all that really matters during our existence in this ever-so-human body of ours, is Love ... is God ... and this can be fully realized in this moment. So, as we try to find an escape from pain, confusion, and suffering, then remember that our pets just might know something that you can't quite understand. Admittedly, dogs and other animals are also capable of fear, jealousy and so on, but they have usually certainly learned the lesson of giving and receiving love unconditionally, which comes through their ability to fully *live in the moment*. So, I am not saying to follow their lead; I am saying, pay attention to how they are living. They ask for love, and in return they get it back. If you were to ask for love, what do think would happen? If you *live in the moment*, then you are asking for love. And if you ask for love, you will receive it because you will be open to experiencing it. There is no greater gift than this.

After reviewing the concept of our animals tending to live

in the moment, let's focus on how living in the moment can change our perspective. I have worked with people who are blind or visually impaired. Through this work I have learned a lot about our own human tendencies when approaching another person. Would you say it is generally true that when a person you do not know approaches you, you initially form an opinion of that person visually? If not, good for you! My point here is that a person who is blind does not have the opportunity of visually forming an opinion of a person before getting to know someone. In my experience, people who are blind have an advantage over people who are sighted in this respect because it is our natural instinct to "judge a book by its cover." We are always told to "not judge a book by its cover," but guess what ... we are judging constantly based on what we are seeing, and creating our own perception that reflects our final opinion of another human being. Does that seem fair to you? It is funny because we judge, yet we hate to be judged. Every moment is an opportunity to paint something different on a brand new canvas.

So, how can living in the moment change our perspective? The answer here is very simple. When we live in the moment, we approach every person and every situation as it is, not as we expect it to be and not how we want it to be. If we all allowed each other to live as we are, as separate souls treading our own path, it would be a truly beautiful world. The reality is that the world is what it is, and the challenge is not how we can change the world, but how we can change our own world. When we take the initiative to love ourselves then we find that the world around us changes. The energy that we resonate from ourselves affects those around us. So, if we live in the moment, accepting ourselves as we are, then we will begin to see that we will accept others as they are, on their own path. If we live with this intention and this perspective, we will find that love is easy to come by because we will be perceiving what people are, not what people should be.

The most important part of finding *the moment* is to find the Divine within ourselves. Brett Dennen says it best in a song of his own, "See, when you forgive your imperfections, and you've auctioned all your clothes, and look to see your true reflection, you will be the one who loves you the most." We need to accept that our imperfections are those that the world has placed on us. In the reflection of the One that created us all, there is only perfection. In order to love ourselves, we must let go of our earthly expectations, see our true reflection, and then find that our love for ourselves is strong enough to pour into every individual that we come across. In finding the moment, your perspective will change ... in acknowledging your perfection, you will find the perfection of others ... and in letting go of what is not true about you, you will find the essence of this God, this Higher Power, this eternal Being. In order to begin falling in love with who we are, it is important to let go of our minds and what we have been told, and discover our hearts (our wants and desires for ourselves).

# CHAPTER 4

## Let Go of Your Mind and Find Your Heart

*Life is beautiful ... nothing less and nothing more ...*
*simplicity is before us, in our own hands ...*

The concept of letting go of your mind and finding your heart may seem a cliché or far-fetched. The truth of the matter is that when you begin to let go of the past, the future, expectations from others, and expectations of yourself, you begin to find that your mind can be keeping you from loving who you are. If *you* cannot love who you are, then who can truly love you? All the knowledge in the world can bring you wealth, but it cannot bring you *true* wealth. I may know everything there is to possibly know, and I may read every book there is to read, but, if I am not experiencing the beauty of every moment, then my knowledge means nothing for my purpose … it is just knowledge. Application of knowledge leads to unveiling the truth; and not being afraid of what is to come on your path comes through beginning to apply what you already know from this book.

In letting go of your fears, you must first establish what your fears are, what you are trying to control and the cultural stigmas that you have claimed as your own. When you do this you are enabling yourself to see what is yours and what is not yours. This gives you a sense of freedom and the ability to differentiate between who you are and who you are not. Once you can identify what seems to be holding you back from peace and joy, you will find that you can only change yourself and not anyone else. The final part of this chapter will discuss how you can distinguish the difference between what is yours and what is someone else's.

Establishing fears, facing control and letting go of cultural stigmas is a process that helps you live in *the moment*. What are you afraid of? Let me begin by sharing my fears with you and perhaps you can relate to these. I am afraid of dying, I am afraid of failing, I am afraid that I will never be enough. Sound familiar? If not, maybe you are afraid of being alone, maybe you are afraid of not being loved, maybe you are afraid that because you are not pretty enough you will never do anything productive, or maybe you are afraid that your beliefs are not the right beliefs. Perhaps you are afraid of being abandoned. Maybe you are afraid that your dreams are only "dreams" and can never become a reality. Maybe you are afraid that you will never be able to pay off your debt and give your family what you want them to have. If none of these fears resonate with you, maybe you are afraid that someone is going to take advantage of you, or you are afraid of being vulnerable, or possibly you are afraid of what might happen. Whatever your fear is or whatever your fears are, they are legitimate because they are YOURS. Claim them, own them, and scream them out loud!

In determining my own fears, I have found peace. I have shaken hands with my fears and allowed them to be my friends, and if my fears are my friends rather than my enemies then we can work together to establish what is true, of this moment, and of the Divine and what is not. I have found that my fears are a part of me because I allow them to be. When I am afraid of something, I first ask myself, why am I afraid? And the answer is always that I am NOT living in the moment, that I am not living in love. Because I am afraid of dying, when I fear death or think about death I am either living in the past (when someone close to me has died) or in the future (fearing that I might die or that someone else I love might die). When the fear of failing comes up for me, then again, I know that I am not living in the moment and that I am doubting who I am... a beautiful and creative person who is talented and worthy. In analyzing this fear of failing I find that I am afraid of what might happen. For instance, I might be thinking that I might not get that job, or wondering what would occur if this did not happen the way I want it to. The truth is that the fear of failure is a state of mind that we humans have imposed on one another. It really does not matter what happens when you live in the moment because you are living as you are, and if you live as you are, then there is no such thing as failure. The lie is that failure matters, and the truth is that it does not matter. Failure is a false truth that we all place on our own shoulders as expectations of the world; the fear of failure does not exist in the creative genius that is within us! Finally, whenever the fear of not being enough arises, then I find that my peace and harmony seem to be out of balance. I always know when I have allowed this fear to creep in because I start to question who I am. However, by reverting back to living in the moment I find the Divine again; I find me again, and all is well. For example, in writing this book I have at times felt that I have not experienced enough (because I am 25 years old) and that I have no business in telling people what is true and what is not true.

When I am living in doubt I question my capabilities, but when I live in the moment and when I love who I am, these words come so expressively and easily. My creativity and my talents are exactly what I allow them to be. I get to control what I think about, and when those fears find a way into my head, then I must find a way to get back to the moment. Sometimes all it takes is listening to a CD that I love, but establish whatever gets you into a mood that is of peace and joy and use this for when your fears come up. Fears are always a result of conditioning from the past or focusing on the future... they are never felt or met with when fully living in the moment.

Another important point to emphasize is that our fears are also a part of us because we have a need to control. I would say that my fear of death is also a result of not being able to control when I might die or when another might die. I can do all I can to prevent it from happening, but, guess what... it is going to happen anyway, and by paying all this attention to it I am missing out on what is in front of me at this moment. How readily we allow ourselves to sink into our fears, and the need to control is so evident in the way that we compare ourselves to others. For example, if I feel that I am not enough physically, then someone whom I think is very pretty will soon become an object of judgment or someone that I do not feel worthy enough to know because I am not happy with who I am. Or, let's say that you do not feel that you are rich enough, then someone whom you think does have enough money will soon become an object of judgment and you may say, "They are just a spoiled brat." This is your fear speaking, which brings about a need to control. Eventually all it boils down to is that you do not love yourself and that you do not feel as though you deserve to be loved. On the contrary, my friends, you are enough, you are worthy, and you are deserving of joy, peace, and happiness. All of these gifts are already within us, and they are yours if you want them.

Part of our development as human beings is learning to deal with our fears and establishing when we are trying to control an outcome. The trick is to establish what our fears are and when we are trying to control events, so that when they do come up (the warning sign is when you do not feel happy) you can move faster into the moment and become better at letting go:

Letting go does not mean to stop caring;
 it means I can't do it for someone else.
Letting go is not to cut myself off;
 it is the realization I can't control another.
Letting go is not to enable;
 but to allow learning from natural consequences.
Letting go is to admit powerlessness;
 which means the outcome is not in my hands.
Letting go is not to try to change or blame another;
 it is to make the most of myself.
Letting go is not to care for, but to care about.
Letting go is not to fix, but to be supportive.
Letting go is not to judge, but to allow another
 to be a human being.
Letting go is not to be in the middle arranging the outcome;
 but to allow others to affect their own destinies.
Letting go is not to be protective;
 it is to permit another to face reality.
Letting go is not to deny, but to accept.
Letting go is not to nag, scold or argue,
 but instead to search my own shortcomings
 and correct them.
Letting go is not to adjust everything to my own desires,
 but to take each day as it comes and cherish myself in it.
Letting go is not to regret the past, but to grow
 and live for today.
Letting go is to fear less and live more ...

       Author Unknown

The culture and the media around us says that material objects will bring us happiness; that money and fame make people better and more worthy; and that if you are not skinny enough, smart enough, or capable enough, then surely you cannot be happy and you are definitely not worth loving. If this is all so true, then why does sitting in a park, not spending any money, and watching what is around me seem so beautiful? Or why does even sitting in a shopping mall not spending any money, and watching what is around me seem to be so beautiful? The answer is simple. If I approach anything as it is, then beauty is not something you look for, it just appears. As a result of the cultural conditioning that we have incorporated into our own beliefs and attitudes, it is easy to find even more of a need to control and even more of a need to fear. Again, I am not worthy enough so I must have this or I must have that. All of these concepts go hand in hand and we allow them to establish a false code by which to live our lives and a ruptured belief system that can only lead to fear, a need to control, unhappiness and a lack of peace.

"I wish that my mom would just see where I am coming from." "Why can't my sister understand why I am choosing to do this?" "What makes it so hard for the president to understand this particular situation?" Do any of these questions sound familiar to you? There is something inside us that tells us that we have an ability to change others; however, it is my conclusion through my experiences thus far, that whenever I get an urge to change another, again I am avoiding living in the moment...living in love. Not only am I not living in the moment, I am choosing to place expectations on another's free will to choose. Part of living in the moment is being able to approach another person where they are on their journey.

Isn't it true that we do have the freedom to experience our own realities? Isn't it also true that society tries to take away our freedom to be who we truly are with its expectations that we are "normal"? Every day we are tested in a choice, to be who we are, or to be what everyone else expects us to be or wants us to become. Once we realize who we are then the choice is easier to make; however, the pressure of the outside world still exists in a very profound and challenging way.

Whether a person is homeless, schizophrenic, a lawyer, in the middle of a divorce, has just experienced a loss, or has a disability, then the approach should not change. If it does, then society has taken over your own perception in one way or another. To be in the present and to meet a person as they are, is to meet God as presented; therefore, to give the other an opportunity to be free. To experience God, to live in the moment, is to let go...to give up control…thereby allowing yourself to see things exactly how they are, not how they should be or once were.

For example, let's say that I approach a person who is homeless and this person asks me for money. I can either walk by and ignore this individual or I can say, "Sure, no problem." What do you usually do? I have sat back and watched people's reactions to people who are homeless (I think it is important to say a person who is homeless, rather than a homeless person; or a person who is blind, rather than a blind person, and so on. Why? Because we should always put the person before their circumstance or condition, because ultimately the circumstance or condition is a label, not who that person is), and it is clear that most people walk by ignoring the fact that this individual even exists. If you don't have any money, why not at least smile? If a particular person who is homeless approaches me, then it is my duty to not judge this person as to why they need money or what they are going to use the money for. When I approach a person as they are, there is no judgment, and there is no need for me to try and change this person's circumstance. What if the person is perfectly happy being homeless? So, the point here is, we really have no business trying to change other people because it is their life, their dreams, their aspirations, their journey, not ours. Do you want to be changed?

There's no harm in offering what works for you, if, through love, you think it could help others—as long as there are no judgments regarding the other person's need for change or any expectations that they will change. Keep in mind that none of us are here to change one another; rather, we are here to love and offer ideas that may help lead to truth. The purpose that I feel is important for me to fulfill is one that presents what I know to be true for me in hope that it may give you or anyone else an opportunity to grow. I am reminded of a quote that states the importance and the power of your own truth:

> Go on your own way, on the path you select for yourself, corresponding to your own innermost inclinations. Don't accept any statement because I made it. Even if it is true a hundred times over, it is still not your truth, it is still not your experience and it will not belong to you. Bring truth into being, and then it will belong to you. Regard the lives of those who have achieved truth only as proof that the goal can be reached.
>
> Elizabeth Haich

Meeting a person where they are, is one of the greatest and most difficult approaches to take as a human being, because we ourselves want to live in the past and in the future. In focusing on these while ignoring the present moment, we automatically assume, judge, and forget what is important in encountering another. To live in harmony and to live in peace is to make a conscious decision that you are who you are and everyone else around you is exactly who they are, and to let it be. When you start to allow other people their own freedom, then you get to experience freedom within yourself and within the relationship you have with that person.

Distinguishing the difference between what is yours and what is not is another important part of recognizing and living in *the moment*. It seems as though the people around us are always expressing what they think is right or wrong, what is true or untrue, and what is fact and what is fiction. At times it gets really difficult to determine what beliefs are yours and what beliefs you have acquired from another person. For example, I have heard many times from different people that there is only one way to pray. As a young person, I always thought that in order to be with God I needed to find the quietest place of all, kneel down, and talk at this much larger than life being that is out there somewhere. I am not stating that prayer is of any negative nature; in fact, it is a very beautiful way of expressing oneself in a spiritual sense and maintaining a sense of peace. I do participate in prayer, meditation, or stillness each and every day, but it is not MY belief that I must be on my knees to do so. I believe that every thought is a prayer...wherever I am and whatever I am doing is a way of expressing myself spiritually. Plus, prayer is also meditating, prayer is hoping, prayer is believing, prayer is the expression of your very existence. Getting on your knees to pray has the same affect as praying in another way, and to me, it does not matter how you do it, or even that you consciously do it. It is your peace, not mine. In saying this, I am attempting to get across the fact that there are many ways to get to the same goal—to happiness—because we all serve a different purpose on this earth.

Once you have established your fears and welcomed in new ideas for dealing with those fears, then you have begun separating yourself from the demands/requirements of others. This helps us to recognize our own purpose so that we may better serve the world. Again, it is always pertinent to remember that we cannot change anyone but ourselves, and in recognizing this it is easier to distinguish the difference between what is ours and what is not ours. For instance, someone once told me that it is not okay for people to be in homosexual relationships. In fact, I have so often heard it said that if a person is in a homosexual relationship they will go to hell. If you are the person being condemned, then this cannot feel too good. What if it was popular belief that being a heterosexual is not okay and that if you are heterosexual you are going to hell? This is a very sensitive but real issue. To be quite honest, why is this an issue at all? Really, why does it even matter? The validity of what I am saying is not to take away from another person's beliefs, rather it is to challenge everyone to think about what is important, and the importance of how another person chooses to live their life is of no hindrance to your Truth.

The point here is that we have to find a way of letting go of what the world has told us and to start paying attention to what our heart is saying. The essence of our Higher Power ... of Love ... is love. When we let go of our fears, establish our issues of control, clarify the cultural stigmas we have placed and kept as our own, let go of trying to change others, and are able to differentiate between what is ours and what is not ours, then we can really begin to fall in love with who we are. When we start paying attention to loving ourselves we start to find peace, and with that peace, we find that the world does not seem so dark ... in fact, we find that there is so much light and that we want to be a part of it eternally:

> Now is the only time. How we relate to it creates the future. In other words, if we're going to be more cheerful in the future, it's because of our aspiration and exertion to be cheerful in the present. What we do accumulates; the future is the result of what we do right now.
>
> Pema Chodron

Why not live in love? Why not live with peace in our hearts? Are you not tired of fighting unending fights? Take a step back, let go of your mind and gain your heart. Gain your heart and be fulfilled in Love…in God…in your Higher Being…YOURSELF.

*How is it that we so easily lose sight of our simple essence?*
*Isn't it true that a person's simplicity never really disappears?*
*We just forget to see it initially. One's own perceptions change*
*the simple ways of one's heart, one's attitude, one's own energy.*
*It is also true that if I am familiar with my own peace,*
*then I can more willingly envision the peace of another.*
*And if I can present myself as the same in all conditions,*
*then others will wonder where they can find THAT peace.*
*I cannot give answers…only LOVE.*

# CHAPTER 5

## Loving Yourself

*CLAIM yourself ... own yourself ... LOVE yourself ...*

T he eternal question is ... how do I love myself? It is so easy to walk through life trying to define our sadness or uneasiness; never allowing ourselves to recognize that we are simply not fulfilling our inward desires, our purpose. I have seen so many people blame their sadness on their spouse or partner, mother or father, brother or sister, without ever admitting that they are truly unhappy with who they are. One of the most important lessons I have learned in my life is that no one can ever love me enough to make me love myself and I can never love anyone enough to make them love themselves. When you are able to recognize this and admit its truth then you are ready and willing to fall in love with your own heart. I know that it sounds strange, fall in love with my own heart? I remember when I first heard this concept. I thought, isn't it arrogant to be in love with myself? I eventually comprehended that falling in love with myself does not make me arrogant, it makes me aware. It does not make me self-centered, it humbles me. Could I become arrogant or self-centered? Sure. But, that means that I do not truly love who I am.

Part of loving yourself is discovering who you are, and the truth of the matter is, you will always be rediscovering who you are. With every new situation, or with every new person that enters your life, there is going to be something, somewhere, that is going to make you clarify what your beliefs about yourself and life are. What can stay constant is your attitude about life and making a choice to take on the ability you have to make this physical world something that is similar to what you would want heaven to look like. With the concepts that have been discussed so far, it is safe to say that living in the moment is part of discovering your own true colors, and if you can find the moment in every moment then there is no need to look any further … you will simply be conscious of what is, not what might be and not what was. One of my goals in life is to be able to look in the mirror everyday and be proud of what I am looking at. If I find something that does not seem appealing regarding my body, then there is something inside myself that I need to discover and let go of. I want to look in the mirror and see beauty and be satisfied with what is before me, and the only way to make that happen is to dive into my soul and find out what it is saying to me. My father always said that if you have a burning desire in your heart, it is God talking to you. I agree. Listen to your heart and what it is telling you ... that is the Divine part of who you are, and it is perfect.

Through this discussion of learning to love ourselves, try to write down all of the lies that you have been told about who you are and the lies you have created along the way because you have not felt good enough about who you are. My lies are as follows: I am not old enough to write a book, as I do not have enough experience; I am not worthy enough to publish a book because I am not good enough; I am not worthy enough to be accepted as a writer about these specific topics because I have had poor judgment in my past; I am not smart enough; I am not pretty enough; I am not funny enough ... the list goes on and on because the lies we tell ourselves never end.

After writing your list, turn them around with affirmations. For example, I would say, I am old enough to write a book, I do have enough experience. I am worthy enough to publish a book and I am good enough … I am MORE than good enough. I am worthy enough to be accepted as a writer because it is part of my purpose. I am smart enough, I am beautiful, and I am funny! I am perfect! We have all been taught along the lines that we are imperfect and that we must deal with and accept our imperfections. If we believe we have "imperfections" then we leave no room to accept our "perfections". We leave no room to see the divine part of who we are. So, this process is not about finding what is imperfect about you (imperfections are defined by society); it is about finding what is absolutely beautiful about who you are!

**Finding your gifts**

Let me tell you a story. In Henderson, Kentucky, in the year of 1910, my great-great-great-grandfather was out plowing his field when something very odd happened along his route. From the sky fell a strange piece of metal. He walked over to pick it up and on it read, "The world will end in 1910." He kept the piece of metal and went about his business.

The very next day the exact same thing happened. My

great-great-great-grandfather was out plowing his field when a similar piece of metal fell from the sky and hit his plow. He went to pick up the piece of metal and again it said, "The world will end in 1910." Puzzled, he kept the piece and finished his job for the day.

The strange thing about both of these incidents was that there was a chance that Haley's Comet was going to hit the earth in the year 1910. But, what ended up happening was that my great-great-great-grandfather died in the year 1910, so his physical world really did end.

My family went on to give these pieces of metal to the government for testing. After being analyzed, the pieces were confirmed to have no similarity to any other metal on the face of the earth. The pieces are still kept within my family.

What does this story have to do with helping you find your gifts? Absolutely nothing; I just wanted to give you a mental break. I thought it was a pretty good family story, and I wanted to share it. Anyway, let's get back to the matter of finding our gifts.

Look, the reality is, in order to fall in love with who you are, it is important to find what your gifts are. There is nothing more fascinating than doing what you love to do! So, the question is, what is it that you love to do? What is it that

YOU want to do? For me, sitting here and writing this book gets me in trouble because I lose track of time. However, that is a beautiful thing! When I sat down and thought long and hard about what I want to do and what I truly enjoy doing, I realized that writing is it, because of my inability to know what time it is while I'm writing. Find something for you in which you lose track of time, find something that you enjoy doing so much that you are not constantly looking at your watch. Find something that gives you an even better opportunity to live in the moment. If you can live in the moment, then you can love yourself, and if you can love yourself, then your gifts will shine. "What you love is a sign from your higher self of what you are to do" (Sanaya Roman).

"To find out what one is fitted to do, and to secure an opportunity to do it, is the key to happiness" (John Dewey). A friend of mine once told me that I already knew deep inside what it is that lights a fire inside me. Since I was a little girl, I have known that writing books that will help people lead a more peaceful life and that standing up in front of crowded rooms speaking about these books would be a part of my life. I am just starting out, but the journey right now is beautiful. My expertise has been in the field of disability and counseling, but it is experiences gained in this particular field that have brought me to this moment... sitting at this desk, writing this book. I do not know what is to come, but I am not afraid; rather, excited. In order to secure an opportunity to go on and do what I am really fitted to do, it is important that I first try it and see what manifests from my efforts. If I am wrong about my purpose, I have only spent some time gaining another valuable experience... but, if I am right about my purpose, then I have got something going here that is worth paying attention to.

Some people say that they are not creative, and that they do not have any special talents. You might be one of those people, but remember that there is no definition for creativity. You may think that since you cannot draw a picture or match your clothes accordingly that you do not have a creative bone in your body. It is all a matter of perception. If you think you are not creative, then guess what, you are not creative. Try to think of creativity as *your* self-expression rather than that of someone else. Your creativity is part of you... and remember, you are beautiful! So, if you want to express yourself by writing codes for a website, bagging groceries at a grocery store, or standing up for your clients as a lawyer, then you are creative. We are all creative... you just have to believe that you are creative, interesting, loving, and worthy of being loved. We are always, and I am guilty of this, waiting for other people to tell us what we are good at. When we do this, we are allowing people to tell our story for us.

Don Miguel Ruiz has said, "We humans have no idea what we really are, but we know what we are not. We create an image of perfection, a story about what we should be, and we begin to search for a false image. The image is a lie, but we invest our faith in that lie. Then we build a whole structure of lies to support it." So, if someone tells you that you would make a great basketball coach and you listen, saying, "Hey, I would make a great basketball coach." Then years into your coaching career you realize that, although you are making a good salary, something just seems out of balance. You begin to question your career and if you want to continue doing what you do. You decide to express your concerns to your closest friends and family, and they then say, you can't quit because you are such a great coach! You believe them. A few years later, you still have that haunting feeling that your purpose is not being fulfilled... and the cycle continues. The point is, we allow others to tell us who to be and we forget to look inside ourselves to find our own gifts. If you are that basketball coach and you have always wanted to be a photographer, then I would say, perhaps you should give it a shot (no pun intended). Or if you are an author and you really want to be a professor, then why not try? Finding our passion gives us a chance to express ourselves as artists, as creators, as individuals seeking to better the world because our light is shining.

## The divine part of you

"That I feed the hungry, forgive an insult, and love my enemy—these are great virtues. But what if I should discover that the poorest of the beggars and most impudent of offenders are all within me, and that I stand in need of the alms of my own kindness; that I myself am the enemy who must be loved—what then?" (C.G. Jung). Falling in love with who we are is not an easy task. In fact, establishing what is holding us back from peace, joy, and happiness is an ongoing challenge throughout life. Sometimes we allow difficulties to take over our outer expressions and we forget to look in the mirror and see the beauty that we possess as individuals. Finding the divine part of ourselves may seem distant, but is right here, right now within our own selves. Our divinity is not defined by other people, nor is it defined by a culture or a society ... it is right inside our own hearts waiting to be given a chance to fly, to experience freedom. If we can free ourselves by expressing our Divine selves, then we are allowing others to experience freedom as well. Be a creator of your own Divine expression.

By living in the moment, letting go of the past and the

future, and finding our passion in life, we can begin to experience our heaven on earth. In our world, many of us are provoked to believe in a higher being that is somewhere in the far-off distance, in the clouds or in the stars. This misconception does not allow us to see the perfection within ourselves. You may say, I am not divine, only God is divine and I am not worthy of divinity. Again, this is another lie ... you are telling yourself that you were not created for a purpose and that you do not have any meaning on this earth. It is my belief that this God, Higher Power, Creator, omnipotent being, however you want to call it, is within each of us, screaming for a chance to shine! PLEASE LET ME OUT! There is no right and no wrong expression of your own personal creations. Whether your greatest excitement is centered around having children and being a stay-at-home mom or dad, or if it is traveling the world to interview specific people, it is your heaven that no one can take away from you unless you allow them to.

Finding what is divine about you and accepting the divine part of you are two separate actions. Although you may have established what you love to do and what you want to do, it is different to actually doing it. Full acceptance of your divine gifts involves you putting those gifts into full expression ... being unafraid of what was and of what will be. You may think that you have to wear a purple robe to be considered Divine, but the beauty of Divinity is its inherent quality of eternity. This gives added meaning to the concept of self-love. Through being divine in origin, it is ours for all eternity. If you choose to be conscious of every moment then falling in love with yourself will come naturally and discovering this overwhelming love for others will forever be imbedded in your everyday life. When you can love for absolutely no reason then you know you have reached a point of clarity ... where it seems that the world is connected to you and that you are a divine part of its existence.

In other words, you are a divine expression on this earth. You are perfect. You are here for a purpose and your heart knows what your purpose is. Let go of the past and the future, and focus on this present moment so that you may find and accept your divinity. Establish the lies you have been told about yourself and let go of what you know is false about you. You are the creator of your life, you are the artist that gets to paint on your own canvas. The world is waiting to be encouraged by your light ... you are worthy of experiencing heaven on earth! "Work while you have light. You are responsible for the talent that has been entrusted to you" (Henri Frederick Amiel).

# CHAPTER 6

## Loving Yourself Means You Love Others

*I love Myself so much*
*That I can love You so much,*
*That You can love You so much,*
*That You can start loving Me*

Rebbie Straubing

It was in a dream that I met a familiar, yet unrecognized, face. I was sitting in a small pickup truck next to a man who appeared to be in his mid-sixties. We were driving down a road that I remember from my childhood in Kentucky, where I spent the first seven years of my life. On the right side there was a ditch that stretched down the entirety of the road until it met with a driveway that led to what looked like a factory with a lot of big machinery. We had just passed a stop light and it was as if our destination was that exact site where people were busy working; however, I found the destination to be unimportant as we began having a conversation.

I felt like I knew this man, but I couldn't quite figure out how I knew him. I asked him how he had been doing and he casually said that he had been doing just fine. He seemed at peace and laid-back. Then, I noticed that he picked up a bottle of medication and he took a pill out and swallowed it. He looked at me and told me that it was for his heart condition. After a few moments of silence, he looked at me very intensely and told me to tell Paula that everything was going to be okay. Then I woke up.

After about an hour of thinking the dream through, the experience still seemed so real that I felt like I needed to tell my mom's good friend, Paula, that everything was going to be okay. I called my mom and I described the dream to her in detail, from the way the man looked, the details of the truck, to the location of the road we were on. And then my mom said, "Oh my, Meagan. That was Paula's father-in-law that came to you in that dream. He died of a heart attack on that very road while he was driving his small pickup truck."

It all clicked for me then. I realized exactly who that man

was. I remembered him after being reminded. I had only met him a few times when I was younger. It was the clues in the dream that gave me a chance to find out who he was: the truck, the heart medication, and the surroundings. So, I told my mom to call Paula and to tell her what had happened and that her father-in-law had told me to tell her that everything is going to be okay. So, my mother called her.

In tears, Paula told my mom that she had been on her knees the night before crying because she was having a very rough time in her life. She said that what she was going through was really hard and that she needed an answer that she was being heard. So, her father-in-law had come to me to get to her so that she could have peace again, to know that she was being heard, that she wasn't alone.

We are never really alone.

Learning to love yourself is not a task that you ever have to do on your own. Sometimes it is more than useful to ask for help. It is okay to say, "Could you please remind me that everything is going to be okay?" Somehow we always interpret *giving* as a sign that we love who we are, but it is the *receiving* that proves how comfortable we are in our own skin. In the above story, Paula needed an answer, and she got one. She was able to receive the comfort she needed by giving her energy in asking for reassurance. The answer came through three different beings to get to her, but it got to her … and it proved to her that there will never be a day in which she will have to walk through life without the love of others being present whether they are alive in body or spirit alone. So, if you can love yourself, then you can ask for help, and when you ask for help, then it will come.

Unhappiness or dissatisfaction is a reflection of how one must feel inwardly. It is true that how simple we perceive life and the world to be depends on the amount of peace we have inside ourselves. There is nothing greater than self-love … if I love myself at all times, then I love others at all times, no matter the circumstance or situation. There is no need to dislike another because if I do, then surely there is something about me that I dislike. There is no judgment in *the moment*. My peace is a mirror image of how I treat all people.

I always ask myself why, if it hurts to be judged, do we judge someone else's story, someone else's pain, or someone else's hopes or dreams with no explanation? If we had the full explanation, surely we would have understanding and compassion rather than judgment and criticism. The greatest gift we can give to one another is the gift of acceptance, the gift of understanding, by allowing someone an opportunity to be exactly who they are. So, truly, we are all different in some earthly capacity. Eventually, with the help of love, patience and understanding, we find that this difference provides for our uniqueness... our difference is okay... our difference is who we are... and that it is perfectly fine... that it is perfectly beautiful. Step back and see what is truly important in your day-to-day existence so that you cannot only understand yourself better, but understand others and where they come from. After all, we are ALL beautiful, and if we understand our own beauty then the beauty of others is more apparent. This creates a clearer picture of what life is about.

When you allow yourself to live in the moment, there is no room for the judgment of others. When you give yourself this most amazing gift then the people around you benefit because you no longer wish that they would make "better" decisions. Instead, you are happy that they are living on their own journey just as you want to live yours. Again, live in the moment so that you can love yourself, and by loving yourself you will see that the world becomes much more beautiful. Every individual will begin to stand out as an individual, not a category and not a label of some sort. Just as you want people to see you for who you are, other people are asking for that same gift. There is something very powerful about giving love without any expectations.

Forgiveness is another important aspect of living in *the moment.* "I will forgive you but I will never forget what happened." Have you ever said this, or have you ever heard this? Forgiveness is one of the toughest and most challenging actions we humans encounter while physically alive. I have seen so many people haunted by not forgiving another person, pushing themselves deep into sadness and despair. Somehow we have learned to put up walls of blame and we succeed in not letting others see who we are through our fear that they just might hurt us too. There are even times when we think we have forgiven a person, and we soon find out that our feelings toward them are still negative, resulting in us still treating them differently. So, is it not safe to say that when we tell someone that they are forgiven, we should truly mean it? This action allows us the freedom to let go and the other person the freedom to continue their life. The question is, how do we forgive someone?

"Then Peter came to Jesus and asked, 'Lord, how many times shall I forgive my brother when he sins against me? Up to seven times?' Jesus answered, 'I tell you, not seven times, but seventy-seven times'" (Matt. 18: 23-24). I think it is reasonably easy for us to understand the freedom that forgiveness brings to all parties involved, but to actually totally forgive another person for betraying you is very tough to complete. Jesus said that we should forgive over and over, no matter how many times one individual has hurt us or betrayed our trust. This is simply an action of complete unconditional love. Easier said than done, right? Remember that although Jesus made a suggestion, forgiveness is your choice, because after all, it is your happiness at stake.

Let me put it this way. I once had a client who had been in a car accident caused by another driver. This accident resulted in her being physically disabled for life, permanently putting her in a wheelchair. This woman appeared to have chosen to be angry at the man in the other car for her entire life. She was an unhappy woman, and she was choosing to be unhappy because she did not want to forgive this man. I understand that this is not an easy task, but for over 30 years she had held on to a grudge that had taken over her attitude and her will to live a full and happy life. She came to me and wanted to know why her relationships were struggling and why she seemed unable to feel fulfilled. I pointed out to her that perhaps she needed to let go of the past and start living for today. It took her a while to grasp what I had said, but in tears, she realized that it was time to let go of the accident and start living her life fully. However, this particular woman had already missed 30 years of her life that she could in no way get back. Do you want to be that person? Every moment is a moment to move forward and let go.

I know that each of us has a person or people who have somehow betrayed our trust along the way. For me, I had many "friends" who turned against me when I told them I was dating a woman, and who pointed the finger and told me that I was going to go to hell. I have met many people who do not want to get to know me after finding out the same information. Many people have wanted to save me from the despair that they perceive would come from living a homosexual lifestyle. Because of all of these misconceptions I was hurt, and left frail and confused. I heard said things such as, "I hate the sin, but I love the sinner," and, "I do not agree with your lifestyle but I love you no matter what." All of these statements seemed double-sided because they somehow went against how I felt about unconditional love. Eventually, I realized that I had experienced a freedom inside me when I decided that I loved who I was and that no one could take that away from me. It took a long time for those statements and misconceptions to not hurt any longer, but I am here, I have let go, I have forgiven, and I am a better person because I am free. Some people may stop reading this book at this point because they do not agree with a same-sex lifestyle, but this is the very point I am trying to make – that you can live your life and I can live mine, and we can all be free of judgment through love and forgiveness. I love myself, and if you love yourself, then me being gay will not be an issue.

Forgiveness is the most powerful and most rewarding outcome of unconditional love. If Jesus taught us one thing, it was that he loved all people exactly the same because he knew he was God's child and he loved who he was, he loved that he was a part of this most amazing creation. We are all part of this creation, we are all perfect. Although we make choices at times that hurt other people, we always have a chance to say "I'm sorry." If you apologize to someone and they do not forgive you, then allow that person to live with their lack of forgiveness and you move on with your life. If you are a person who needs to forgive someone, then give yourself the freedom that comes from letting go and allow yourself to live a full and happy life. When you let go, you will find a peace inside you because you know that you have given the other person their freedom back as well. People make mistakes, in fact you have probably made a few, and that is just the way it is. Try to recognize where you feel uncomfortable and notice if it is something that an act of forgiveness could cure. You cannot truly love yourself if you are holding on to the past ... and part of letting go of the past is forgiving. The truth of the matter is, there is always going to be someone talking about you behind your back, but if you can let go and love who you are and find a way to allow other people to live with their own insecurities, then you are steps closer to finding fulfillment.

We have, so far, established who God or who your Higher Power is to you. We have talked about letting go of the past and the future and the importance of living in the present, at this moment, and only at this moment. The fourth chapter talked about letting go of your mind and finding your heart; how to establish your fears; how you cannot change anyone but yourself; how to claim what is yours and to let go of what is not yours. Chapter 5 talked about loving yourself completely by finding your gifts and accepting the divine part of you. This chapter spoke about loving yourself so that you may love others even more. We have established that there is no judgment if you choose to live in the moment and that you can truly love who you are even more by forgiving and letting go where it is necessary. Ultimately, we must realize that we are all one; we are all on this planet together ... each of us reaching for our own dreams and our own happiness. Let's continue to take steps forward in making our world one by recognizing the beauty inside ourselves. "To forgive is to set a prisoner free and to discover that the prisoner was you" (Lewis B. Smedes).

# CHAPTER 7

## We Are All the Same ... We Are All Connected

*We are all connected to everyone and everything in the universe.
Therefore, everything one does as an individual affects the whole. All thoughts,
words, images, prayers, blessings, and deeds are listened to by all that is.*

Serge Kahili King

My great uncle decided to go hunting on his own one day. In Henderson, Kentucky, this was a very normal thing to do, so my uncle took his truck, his dogs, and his guns to his usual parking spot. Once he had parked, he took his dogs out of their cages, grabbed his guns and walked a few miles to an open field to begin his day of hunting.

As my uncle was walking he began to feel a great pain down his left arm and into his chest: he was having a heart attack. This wasn't the greatest place in the world to have a heart attack, in the middle of a field with no one around to hear his cries but his dogs. He eventually passed out.

When my uncle woke up he was back in his truck. His dogs were in their cages and he was alone. As he was reflecting on what had just happened, he remembered feeling the sense of being carried but of being unable to wake up and see in full consciousness who his rescuing angels were. My great uncle was able to drive his own truck to the hospital and is still alive today.

In the midst of an earth that is overshadowed with physicality, it is so easy to ignore the place where miracles are simply an everyday occurrence A lack of self-love and a failure to recognize that everything in the world is in fact One mean that we easily overlook our connectedness. My great uncle was carried miles from where he had a heart attack to his truck. How do you think this happened? The answer could go so many different ways, but it is not the "how" but the "what" that matters. It is not how my uncle got to his truck, it is the what: the fact that my uncle is alive and able to share this story. Within our connectedness as a human race, no matter how our soul represents itself, the search for realization of our true nature is never really over because each moment clarifies something new for our own purpose. We are continually transforming as a result of life, as a result of circumstances, and as a result of self-discovery. By realizing that we all act together as one giant heartbeat, we too have a chance, and a choice, to experience miracles each and every moment—if we just stop looking and start seeing. Although we can't explain how miracles happen, the matter of why they happen becomes clearer when one sees the underlying connectedness and love that exist between all beings. And maybe that if we can fully tune into this sense of connectedness and be open to all possibilities, then we will see the miracles that are already happening around us all.

As we begin to love ourselves and define who we are and what our purpose is, we discover that the moment holds Love, God, Divinity, in a light that never actually has to disappear. When the truth fades away, then it is clear that our thoughts are tampering with our emotions; our choice to pay attention to those thoughts takes us on a road to nowhere, quickly. Somehow, we always need to know how something happened or why a certain circumstance took place … but, eventually the answers come, with patience, with trust, and with love.

I mentioned us, as a human race, being one heartbeat. You may think, well, Meagan, how can that be when all of our heart rates are different speeds? If you think outside the box, then you might discover and recognize how all things can naturally fall into their place in the heartbeat of the universe. To be in step with the universe, you must first be in step with your Divine self so that you can recognize and fully appreciate your connectedness to others. Have you ever experienced a "good" day, a day when everything just seemed to go right? Those are the kind of days we would like to have all the time, right? Well, guess what, you can ... we can ... I can! What about those days we view as being "bad days"? If we say it is bad, then it will be a bad day, but if we say it is a good day, then God, the Universe, Energy finds a way for all that we want and all that we desire to become a reality.

Have you ever heard "Ask and you shall receive?" Although this may seem imaginative and unrealistic, I really believe that if you do ask, you WILL receive! What does this have to do with our connectedness? As human beings we are all created from the same Source. Although very different in our expressions, somehow we Divinely work together to make the world exactly what it is. If I were to get up one morning and say, "Something great is going to happen today," the chances are that something great would happen that day, not because I expected it to, but because I KNEW it would happen. When we believe in greatness, then we get to experience greatness, due to our ability to follow our heart and articulate our purpose.

As an example of the importance of having trust in the process of life providing for our needs, let me tell you of a time when my parents were at a crossroads in their life ... trying to decide what road would be best for the entire family at the time. I too was in a transition and was about to go off to college and had just experienced the death of a friend.

My mom has proven to be a very faithful believer in prayer and whenever she found herself on her knees for answers they would naturally come. I believe that this is because she knew answers would come when the timing was right. At this particular moment in my parents' life, my mom found herself asking for an answer. But, this time, she asked for a specific sign ... a bird, a specific bird at that ... a cardinal.

As my parents were sitting outside talking about whether or not to sell their current house, a cardinal flew and nestled on the chair between them, looking at them as if the answer couldn't be any clearer. The next day my parents put the house up for sale and it sold on that day! This story beautifully resonates with the truth of the saying that if we ask, we shall receive. No matter how we ask, how we give, or how we receive, the answers are always manifested when you know they will manifest. When you throw your energy, your prayers, your questions out to God, to Love, to Energy, to your Higher Power, with confidence that the answer will be revealed, then truly, what is it that can stand in the way? I have to say, only I myself can stand in the way of my own receiving. If a situation seems unclear or uncomfortable, then it is up to me to discover the discomfort. The answer might be right under my nose or within my heart, but if I fail to listen or to be open, then the answer evades my grasp and I am left to blame that which I thought had not answered my question. A difficult challenge in life is claiming what I can control and taking control of it, and then letting go of what I need to let go of while trusting in the process that WILL take place.

So, what is the relationship between giving and receiving? I like to think of giving and receiving as a boomerang effect. What you give is what you get. Giving and receiving is an abundant part of life. Are you the type of person that loves to give because it makes you feel good? If so, that is great! On the other hand, are you the type of person that is willing to receive when someone wants to give something to you? I have to admit that I am a person that loves to give, but has a hard time receiving. Why is this so? Maybe I think that other people are worthy to receive and I am not. Or maybe

I feel as though I am too good to receive, so pride is getting in my way. No matter the reason why, I have a difficult time receiving... and when I do not accept help, then I stop the flow of life—I threw the boomerang, but I did not allow it to come back. Through turning down someone's kind gift, whether it be monetary, of time, ideas or compliments, I stop the expression through which that person is attempting to define their purpose and existence. Life is a circle, a circle that is not supposed to ever end. From now on when you give something to someone else, notice what it would feel like if that person did not accept your gift, your compliment, or your kind gesture. When we stop the flow of love, then we are stopping the flow of connectedness.

If willing and able, think of the world as a place that just keeps spinning and that everything, everyone has a purpose ... and that in order for people to find joy, then full expression must be allowed. If your purpose and meaning is important, would you not believe that the person next to you also has a meaning and purpose that is to be conveyed by none other than themselves? The degree of our connectedness to one another is what either stops the flow of life or allows the flow of life to explode in beauty! To be good givers, we must also be good receivers. As we learn to love ourselves and express our purpose, then we find that receiving becomes easier and that it comes in many forms.

A few years ago, I got a call from my mom that her best friend was in the hospital. My mom's friend of 30 years, Ann, had been sick for almost a year with lung cancer, pneumonia, and brain damage from the pneumonia. My mom and the doctors were convinced that this was my last chance to see Ann because she would not live much longer. So, I got in my car and drove the three hours to see her. My parents were already there when I arrived. My mom was very upset. My dad was trying to comfort my mother while dealing with his own hurt.

Although I had known Ann my entire life and we shared a special connection, I did not know any of her extended family until that night in the hospital. Once I arrived, my dad, mom and I went into the hospital room where Ann was lying in bed. We were told that she had not been responding coherently all day. As we walked in, she recognized us immediately and got really excited. She was coherent for several minutes, asking questions about the family and what was going on. At this point in her disease and indeed for the past year, her being conscious of people around her was practically unheard of. We got to see Ann as Ann for only a few minutes, but that was enough ... that was the miracle.

As I said my goodbye, unsure as to whether to hug her, cry, or smile, I stood at the end of her bed and stared into her eyes as if to say "See you later." Ann looked me straight in the eyes, completely coherent, and, as if there were no one else standing in the room, she said, "Goodbye." I felt a lump in my throat because I knew that was the last time I would see her. That night I drove home thinking of what had just happened and the impact that it had on my heart. I thought of all of those whom I had already lost in my life and what I had gained from those deaths along the way.

I got home later that night and with complete silence in my house, no roommates and no distractions, I stayed up and felt that I was being told to write Ann's eulogy. So, I wrote Ann's eulogy and I put it away. Three months later Ann died. I woke up the morning that she died realizing that I had dreamt of heaven and knew that Ann had passed away. I waited for my mom to call and confirm, and when she did I remembered that I had written Ann's eulogy three months before. I began to question whether to let Ann's family know that I had written something or to just keep it to myself. Not only did a cardinal appear before me as I was thinking about doing the eulogy or not, that same night Ann came to me in a dream and asked me to speak at her funeral. Even without knowing any of her family, I called my mom the next day and asked her to call Ann's family to see if it would be okay if I spoke. They graciously accepted my offer and placed me as the second of three speakers.

Once my family and I arrived at the funeral, I began to get nervous because I realized that I did not really know anyone well other than my own family members and I wondered what people would think of me speaking. As I was sitting there waiting for the funeral to begin, I felt Ann's presence on the front row and I was comforted with that feeling. The service began, my turn came, and at the end of the eulogy this is what came splurging out of my mouth: "I cannot know the ways of the wind—I cannot know the brightness of the sun—BUT, I know that today I get to witness the celebration of an angel's continuing presence in my life and in yours."

After I finished speaking, I sat down and a woman began to sing "Wind Beneath My Wings" without prior knowledge of what I was going to say. As soon as the song began, the wind blew the church's side-door open and a spotlight of sunshine beamed onto Ann's only daughter as if Ann's spirit had gotten up and left the church. Everyone saw it and everyone broke into tears at that moment, simply because the sight was absolutely astounding. Who could have predicted that the last sentence of my eulogy would come to signify something so powerful for Ann's family and friends? This moment was beyond me ... I was only a muse to a creation surpassing knowledge and understanding. We are all truly connected ... we are all truly ONE ... our spirits live.

When someone dies or when we experience loss in any fashion, it is our physical existence that challenges our perspective on our way of dealing with that loss. When we lose a person who is close to us or someone who has somehow served a purpose on our path, then we cannot help but grieve the missing touch that was once there. Throughout my life, I have been offered many experiences with people who have physically moved on ... them sending me messages for others, their finding ways to communicate through me with those who are still on this earth. What does this mean? To me, this means that although we physically lose others, we do not really lose their love, their support, or their impact. Somehow, we all communicate on a level that is purely Divine and eternal. So, how do we deal with loss?

As my mom and I were standing before Ann's coffin at her funeral, I told my mom, "You are giving Ann a great gift by dealing with her loss rather than her dealing with your loss." Viktor Frankl would say that it is a matter of perspective when we deal with life, and it is that perspective that will either carry us forward in growth or keep us complacent in our steps. The fact of loss is that we never really lose ... we just transform; as we transform through grief, the person who has died transforms into a world separate from that we can see, but one of which we are still truly a part of. The more we can recognize that the world is a small part of the universe, the more we begin to visualize everything, rather than just part of the big picture. Yes, we do lose physical contact with people throughout our lives (and as you know, it just does not feel that great), but we never, ever have to lose a spiritual connection ... that connection lives on and on. Our relationships take place in different forms. Yes, we will cry when we miss someone, but we can also be comforted in knowing that the Divine Love which encircles the universe will always hold us in the utmost continuation of life by transforming our spirits and shaping that which is already here. We are truly perfect in any form, and we are learning that perfection means change, means love, means understanding that all is well.

## CHAPTER 8

### There is No Controversy in Truth

*Believe nothing just because a so-called wise person said it.*
*Believe nothing just because a belief is generally held.*
*Believe nothing just because it is said in ancient books.*
*Believe nothing just because it is said to be of divine origin.*
*Believe nothing just because someone else believes it.*
*Believe only what you yourself test and judge to be true.*

Buddha

What is truth? A common dictionary definition of truth is "agreement with fact or reality." There are also many other perceptions of truth created by different people who have lived dissimilar lives and have chosen to be writers, photographers, coaches, teachers, doctors, etc. In one simple statement, I affirm that only you can know your truth, because you are the carrier of what is true for you. You are the only representative for your life! When you are able to claim your truth, your purpose, your reason for being on this earth, then you will find that there is no controversy regarding your truth because your desires, your dreams, and your passions are being expressed and lived.

As children we begin to learn what our parents believe, what our peers think, and what our teachers feel is important. For instance, I remember when a friend of mine told me that there was a monster in an old house in our neighborhood. From then on, I used to run by that house when I was walking home from school. I lived in fear each and every day because I had allowed myself to be deceived. I remember thinking, "Now, I know I saw an older woman in that yard the other day, but if my friend says there is a monster, then there must be a monster in that house." Although, as children, we somehow know when something feels uncomfortable to us, we still find a way to make another's perspective "right" in our own minds. Perhaps, we do this because we are not sure what is true for us yet, or maybe we want to be accepted by adopting someone else's perspective of the world, someone else's truth. As we grow older and are exposed to other perspectives, then we begin to develop a voice for what feels good to us personally.

When we start to believe in ourselves as effective, purposeful, and creative beings, then we discover what is important to our truth ... our perspective ... our originality.

One of the most extraordinary parts of life is that we have a choice to express ourselves as we choose. We all have an opportunity to see the world as a place of beauty or as a place that is constantly against us. We each have our own unique truth which is diverse from everyone else's. Self-discovery is constantly transforming, and with every decision we have to make we are given a chance to define our truth further, to grow in greater ways, and to express our creativity on different levels. If I acknowledge that I am unique, love my uniqueness, and embrace my passions, then there is truly no controversy within myself. The more I am able to live in my truth then the more everyone around me is free to live his or her truth as well. This little story shows how we tend to see what we expect/are conditioned to see rather than the truth of a situation:

Word spread across the countryside about the wise Holy Man who lived in a small house atop the mountain. A man from the village decided to make the long and difficult journey to visit him. When he arrived at the house, he saw an old servant inside who greeted him at the door.

"I would like to see the wise Holy Man," he said to the

servant. The servant smiled and led him inside. As they walked through the house, the man from the village looked eagerly around the house, anticipating his encounter with the Holy Man.

Before he knew it, he had been led to the back door and escorted outside. He stopped and turned to the servant, "But I want to see the Holy Man!"

"You already have," said the old man. "Everyone you may meet in life, even if they appear plain and insignificant, see each of them as a wise Holy Man. If you do this, then whatever problem you brought here today will be solved."

As is expressed here, the truth that was overlooked is that we are all Holy as unique and creative individuals.

Living in the moment and loving yourself makes us see our differences as similarities. Deepak Chopra has stated, "The physical world, including our bodies, is a response of the observer. We create our bodies as we create the experience of our world." Our experiences are what we allow them to be. Our differences are mainly made up of physical attributes that are used to distinguish one Spirit from another. Another difference between us all is our purpose in life and the passions we express. We all come from the same Creator, whatever that creator feels like or looks like to you … we do all come from the same Being, the same essence of the universe. Our passions and creative nature may differ from the person next to you, but those passions come from the basis of Love. This is what makes us similar, the fact that our nature desires Love and that we express from that Love.

A few years ago a friend of mine, Eric, committed suicide, and when I heard the news I was surprised because he was such a loving, unselfish human being. I knew in my heart of hearts that there had to be a significant reason as to why he would have decided to take his life at such a young age. The night after I had heard the news I attempted to lay down to get some rest while staying with my parents. I had a feeling that Eric's presence was near me. When I had turned off the light, which it took me a while to do, I rolled over away from the door and toward the window. I found Eric sitting next to the bed looking straight ahead. So, I freaked out, ran to my parents' room and laid in the king size bed with them. With my eyes wide open I could somehow still feel the presence of Eric's spirit. I knew that I would not rest until I was able to let go and experience his entire presence. As I lay there wide awake, he appeared again.

Eric told me that he was okay and that his death had been for good reasons. He clarified that his death would save a lot of his friends from continuing to use drugs and that it would turn a lot of lives around. He did not do it for selfish reasons, but he actually thought before he decided to die that his death would save the lives of others. I was not surprised ... I am not surprised. After the next few days, at Eric's funeral I shared something I wrote after the experience with him that night:

If love can be comprehended, then it simply is not love. He saw, he smiled, he gave, he insisted on finding and loving the beauty in every being that stood in front of him or behind him. Somehow, the equality and fairness that he sought for every person carried forward in acceptance so that he could stand beside them. As children of Love, of the Divine, we have been asked to not only glance at those around us, but to first envision what another person's heart entails. He saw through assumptions, judgments, expectations, and he found what some of us cannot comprehend ... unconditional love for all. His continuing presence ... his spirit ... will show us that we, too, can allow our light to shine by simply embracing ourselves and our differences in order to find complete peace. As humans we are not only hoping for our pain to be eased, but for an understanding of our hurt and a way to be healed. May we heal from this day forward knowing that we have been touched, and that we, too, can love without condition as Eric did. We must not fear what it is that we can give because it is our fears that keep us from any unknown potential. Eric was not afraid ... he did not fear the result of Love ... giving oneself for others.

We all have a message to portray, a passion to develop, and

a life to be proud of. Eric's story shows us that we are all similar in Love...we all want to give and receive of the same substance...abundance. As different as we think we are, we are all truly alike, and there should be no controversy in this truth.

Gratitude is another important aspect of truth that we must consider in our growth as individuals. Imagine a jigsaw puzzle. In fact, picture your life as a jigsaw puzzle. What does it look like? My puzzle has different pieces with various colors, various textures outlined and intertwined with tough times and joyous moments. Just as you can put pieces of a puzzle together, you too are putting pieces of your life together...our lives are like a puzzle. Once you had spent hours putting a puzzle together and it was complete, then what would that puzzle look like if you took a piece away? What if you took a piece of your life puzzle away, would you be who you are right now? Even the most frustrating piece that you just cannot seem to find is still a part of your puzzle. Just as you can choose which puzzle you buy at a store, you too can choose what you want your life puzzle to look like from now on. Yes, we choose to create our own puzzle, our own heaven!

Gratitude may seem simple in its definition (a feeling of thankfulness and appreciation); you may express it by, "I am grateful that I have two legs to walk on," or, "I am thankful for my mom." But, gratitude has a depth and a use that is powerful when used with proper understanding of the circumstances prompting its use. Have you ever heard the American expression "Don't sweat the small stuff"? In other words, it's not worth expending a lot of energy or wasting your time on unimportant or small things. I like to think of this phrase in a different way by saying, "I am thankful for the small stuff." All of the circumstances that have taken place in my life have been meaningful. A good friend of mine once said, "Don't be a victim of circumstance, be a champion of it!" Although there are pieces of my life that have been painful, the pain and that piece of my puzzle is what makes me completely...me. The essence of my heart has endured what it has endured with gratefulness. I am moved beyond words for all of the broken hearts, defeats, and endless moments. But, things do get better and life does continue, and I am grateful for now, having the perspective to see that life can truly be one of heaven. I am thankful for the small, tough stuff that has taken me to right where I stand at this moment. I have found that having gratitude in the present rather than in retrospect has been influential on my growth, on the beauty of my own puzzle.

Somehow, we spend the majority of our time paying attention to other people's puzzles, forgetting to look at our own. Who wants a puzzle that looks like everyone else's? Part of being grateful is stepping away from our irrelevant expectations, and remembering that we are perfect just as we are. When we are able to do all that has been discussed throughout this book (to believe that we are perfect and that we deserve to have a joyous life) then we transform our thoughts and actions with a gratitude of depth by identifying all pieces of our puzzle and being grateful for each piece. Although it is tough to be grateful when someone dies, when someone breaks our trust, or when something does not go our way, if we look hard we can invariably find something to be grateful for and this marks the change in perspective that releases us by simply saying, "thank you." I am thankful for having the time I had with this person, or I am thankful for what they taught me about myself. It is our perspective on the world that makes it beautiful … or not.

A few years ago, I was on my way to the airport with plenty of time to make my flight. With about ten minutes of the drive left, there was a wreck ten cars ahead of me. Traffic was cut off across all five lanes and I was unable to get through. Unfortunately I missed my flight and had to wait in the airport for six hours. I will say that at first I was pretty upset because I was on a set schedule to meet several people in

New York as a part of my curriculum for my Master's degree. I did not feel much better when I realized I had only missed check-in by five minutes. At the time I was not grateful. So, I had to settle for taking the next flight later that day, and that was if I was able to get past "stand-by." I knew that there must be some reason as to why I was to take the next flight so I waited to find out what it was.

During my wait, I was sitting at a Starbucks and decided to pull out a book that I had been given sometime before, *The Alchemist* by Paulo Coelho. I began reading the book and was unable to put it down. After getting half-way through the book I noticed that the chair next to me became available. Within five minutes a man in his mid-forties asked if anyone was sitting there and I told him that there was not. He sat down and I continued reading the book. After about 5 minutes I got up to throw some trash away and take a break from the intensity of the book. As I sat back down he asked me what I thought of the book. I told him that so far it was truly wonderful and that it was having a very positive effect on me.

The man went on to tell me that he had heard of the author and the book, but he was unsure as to why he had never picked it up to read. I told him that it was about the human experience, following our hearts, and the fact that we are truly worthy of our dreams. The reason for my connection with this man was obvious, and I got the urge to tell him that he should pick up the book. We both grew silent for about five minutes, and I went back to reading. He finally stood up and was off to catch his flight. He said that he was happy to have met me and that he would pick up the book and that perhaps it would change his life.

It was then that I realized why I had missed my flight that morning. For some reason, this man needed to hear me tell him to pick up that book. Who knows why or what for ... the reason is unimportant. The moral of the story is that no matter the circumstance, no matter if there is a set schedule or not, there is a purpose behind every situation ... whether it be to grow, to assist another on their path, or for someone to assist you on your path. This is truly what life is about ... the life process ... the cycle of life ... everything affecting everything else in the most profound and mysterious ways. I am now much quicker to say thank you when situations do not seem to go the way I think they should, because there is always a reason, always a purpose behind the connectedness between each of us.

One thing I always ask myself regarding gratitude is, what have I done today to let people know I appreciate them and their beauty? How does it feel when you receive a compliment? If it feels good, then perhaps it feels the same to other people. Since I was little I have realized the importance of saying thank you. The awesome beauty that is before me each and every day...why not say, "You are beautiful and I am thankful for you"? The energy we put out is the energy we get back...remember the boomerang effect? The same is true when it comes to gratitude. If we can sit back and be grateful for what we have rather than wishing for what we don't have, and if we can be grateful for the beauty in every person we come across, and not place expectations on others, then the Love is reciprocated. When we are grateful, then people around us become grateful, and we start to create an environment that is much closer to stepping into heaven.

## CHAPTER 9

### Life Is Meant to Be Simple

*Life is really simple, but we insist on making it complicated.*

Confucius

Two people were wandering around in the desert aimlessly. They didn't know where they were and they were weary. They sat down on a rock, quiet and silent, just sitting, until the one fellow said to his companion, "My brother is lost." And the companion responded, "I am not lost. Only the way is lost. I am here."

Do you ever feel lost? Do you ever feel confused or scared about where your life is going? Do you know what your dreams are, but you just are not really sure how to reach them? These doubts and feelings are with us much of the time, and to add insult to injury we find ourselves inquiring about our potential and if we are good enough to achieve those dreams. Learning to love ourselves is not something that happens over night, but it is something that will happen if we are willing to work on making our lives simpler. After all, as the above story states, we are never really lost ... we just think we are.

You see, we often find ourselves sitting in solitude with thoughts of difficulty and hardship, never realizing that our thoughts and our fears are what make our lives difficult and hard. The truth is, life is simple. If the concepts that have been discussed throughout this book are used in your day-to-day life, then you find that what you have been told throughout your life is still running/ruling your life. You get to say how you will live your life and if you want it to be simple. So, what are you waiting for? If you are waiting for a sign, well, here it is ... now is the moment to turn away from thinking that life is hard and to turn towards believing that it is truly simple. In Love, there is only simplicity. How? I believe that if we live our lives according to our hearts and with a basis in Love rather than in our minds with all our doubts and concerns, life becomes much simpler. Love is the essence of our beings and should be the reason why we get up every day and the reason why we feel compelled to do what we do. It is our true motivation, our encouragement and our purpose in all that we choose to be a part of.

Several years ago I was stuck in a place where I was struggling, trying to find peace and purpose in my life; trying to find peace within my purpose and trying to find my purpose, to say the least. I would walk around trying to please other people, and by doing so I would easily forget who I was. This always caused a temporarily satisfying peace but invariably left me feeling unfulfilled. I think that we all have a tough time trying to find a constant peace within ourselves, but I have begun to find it … I have begun to see hope and understanding by listening to my own Truth.

During one of my toughest moments, after telling my family that I was dating a woman, I needed some reassurance that I was okay just the way I was. It wasn't easy determining the path to my peace until I began to conclude that Divine love is unconditional … that no religion could determine the fate of my spirit after this physical life. I believe that God, the Divine, It, Love is not judgmental; therefore, only I am permitted to determine where my peace lies in collaboration with the Divine and whether to accept the judgments of others.

In the midst of this transition, during a time in which I needed reassurance, a good friend of mine who had recently passed away came to me in a dream. She confronted me face to face, gently hugged me, held my hand and told me that I was perfectly fine the way I was and that I needed to be okay with me. Through the essence of her angelic presence, I knew when I woke the next morning that everything was really going to be okay and that I could stand tall, proud of my own path. Throughout my life, I have been blessed with the healing presence of those who are no longer physically on this earth. It was this experience that carried me into a direction of positive thinking in what seemed like a judgmental world. I realized that I am perfect the way that I am, and that if I follow my heart then my fulfillment will never by in question. The key is to enjoy life...and if you are not enjoying life then perhaps it is time to re-evaluate and listen to what your heart is saying to you. Now, although the world may still be judgmental, I do not see it as judgmental. I see all people and things just as they are...beautiful creations that have a purpose and a gift to express. Life is simple when you love who you are, when you can look in the mirror and smile at what is before you.

**EXPECTATIONS**. Do you have expectations of yourself? Do you have expectations of others? So often we have a set plan for how things should go or how things are supposed to be. We are constantly placing expectations on ourselves, on our relationships, on our jobs, and even on how our sandwich should taste when we go to a restaurant. Particularly in this modern era, the way of life seems to be one of continuous expectations. What happens when expectations are not met? Do you get disappointed, do you get angry, or do you jump for joy when something does not go the way you think it should? I know that when I have tried to make plans for something usually the plans get altered in some form or fashion. Either the weather changes; people cannot make it because they are sick or have changed their minds; or technology is not up to the task in hand. Whatever the reason, my expectations are crushed. The point is that we tend to live on expectations. If we live on expectations then there is no room left in our minds for other outcomes and we are closing the door to other opportunities.

Recognizing that nothing is set in stone and that expectations are prone to leaving you disappointed, presents an opportunity to free yourself even further. Living a life that is simpler involves dropping your expectations and allowing the universe to flow as it will. Instead of going into a situation with expectations of worldly perfection, try and go into a situation with no expectations: you will find perfection in the releasing of pressure, and the flow of life will present itself with clarity.

**BEST FRIENDS FOR EVER**. I had a friend when I was little, and we always said that we would be best friends forever. We were sure at the age of eight that we would always live right down the street from one another, sharing secrets, playing games, and enjoying the sun. Why is it that we have not spoken in the last 12 years or so? Were we not going to be best friends forever? At the age of eight, I was able to live in the moment, and truly, we were best friends in the moments we were together and we could not conceive change in the future. However, change happened and we grew apart .... we chose separate paths, and our paths have not run into one another in a long time. Relationships change because people grow and start to follow their own hearts. Relationships do not remain static, they are dynamic and fluid ... we all change, we all grow, and we all want peace and joy in our lives, and this pushes us to make decisions that will give us only these things. It is okay to change, it is okay to let go, and it is okay for us all to follow that which is our own Truth. There are best friends all around us, in every moment and in every person.

Nothing in this life is stagnant. Permanence is but an illusion of our imagination. You do not have to stay in the job that you are currently in. You do not have to dye your hair brown because grey streaks are coming through. You do not have to go to a specific church or join a particular club because your friends are doing it. The only thing you have to do is live with yourself. In living with yourself, then comfort encompasses you, joy can be a part of your existence, and abundance can be at your finger tips. Know that you are perfect and that your journey is unique and beautiful. Where your heart tells you to go ... go ... and know that all will be laid out before you like a dream, like a piece of heaven. That which created us only wants happiness for us, otherwise what is the purpose of living?

Loving yourself is parallel to distinguishing the difference between negative energy, or energy that does not serve your Truth at a particular moment, and positive energy. Understanding negative energy or learning to live with negative energy is a great tool that will help you to evolve as a human being. Positive and negative energy are both productive for the progression of our personal evolution, and the more enlightened we become then the more we can be with negative energy (because we are strong in who we are and we get back what we give out) and thus help to transform our world. During a person's evolution, there could be times when they choose to walk away from negative energy. The important thing is to be aware of what is happening and understand the effect it is having on you and respecting that you have a choice. I believe that positive energy is love. I also believe that we need both positive and negative energy to make a world and that often positive energy is generated in the midst of much negative energy or suffering. The more you experience joy and the more you become self-realized (recognizing that the heart is filled with love), the easier it becomes to be around anyone—even those who challenge us.

The key for me has been to just be who I am in all situations, and if I can do that, then I am free. When my freedom is exposed to energy that does not serve my truth, then I can gracefully walk by it without knowing that it ever tried to get in, or I can choose to be around it and allow my purpose to shine and not allow that negative energy to bring me to a place where I am doubting who I am. The question is, how do you determine what is negative energy and what is not negative energy? The determination of what negative energy is to you, is finding what actions or choices you make that do or do not serve your Truth, your Purpose. For instance, if my Truth is to serve people who have disabilities, then I would choose to not be around people who believe people with disabilities do not deserve equal rights. Keep in mind that everything is of the Divine; however, what may be true for someone else, may not serve your Truth in a positive way.

Anything that is of Love, of joy, of purpose, of clarification, or of humility and passion is of the Divine … and if something is of the Divine, then the energy is apparently that which can only lift you up. If something is of anger, gossip, arrogance, or at the expense of someone else's life, then you get to choose if partaking in these actions is true for you or if it is not true for you at the time. Anytime you find yourself in fear, living in the past or the future, living with expectations, then unnecessary negative energy is being created by your own choices. When someone else is exposing you to negative energy by talking badly about someone else, then you have the ability to change the subject, walk away, or encourage the conversation to move on. But can someone else really expose us to negative energy? We allow things to happen, right? Yes, although someone can expose you to negative energy, you manifest it as a negative energy in your response, but through awareness you always retain the choice. If you choose to encourage the flow of negative energy, energy that is not serving your Truth, then you will be the one who will suffer. When you talk badly about someone then it is an expression of how you feel about yourself. Try to catch yourself when you are in a situation such as this. Remember that you are a perfect being and that all people are perfect as well. I know this is a hard concept to really master and to grasp, but you will feel so much better when you let go of caring about what other people are choosing to do. When you do this then you can focus on the flow of positive energy and really sink your teeth into living in the light of your Truth.

The energy we give out is the energy that we will receive. I was in line at a store the other day and saw a woman walk up to the counter and blame a clerk for not having a particular product in stock. The clerk must have felt attacked, and although he had the ability to order more of that product (because he did for me), he did not offer that option to this woman. So, what we give people is what they will give us back. If you smile at someone and say hello, chances are that they will smile and say hello back. Your energy is key to the essence of the environment around you. Drop the expectations and realize that nothing is set in stone and you will find that the negative energy you are exposed to will be a breeze to surpass. Life will always throw opportunities at you to decide which you would rather have, either negative or positive energy surrounding you. If you have a business and you surround yourself with positive energy, then don't you think your business will flourish? People want to be loved and if you expose people to love, then they will keep coming back and expressing their love for you.

Energy is a simple way of explaining how we feel about who we are. If I love who I am then I will reflect love on others. I can either build myself up and share my love with the world without saying a word, or I can choose to be a victim, constantly waiting for the world to make my life better. Negativity is just as natural as Love and Love is sometimes too natural for our taste. The Truth is that we were molded by Love, created by Love, and everything that we need to be happy is already here...heaven can really be a part of your world. Walking away from the energy that is not serving you will bless you beyond belief ... your freedom will continue to grow, and you will no longer have to search for your fulfillment.

It is also important in the beginning stages to consider what our spiritual journey and our truth look like to us. When you first consciously embark on your spiritual journey (and in the early stages), you may want to avoid people who emit negative energy, which may bring you down. You get to choose what serves and what does not serve your truth. However, also consider that although a person may emanate negative energy, that does not mean that they are a bad person or any less Divine than you are. No one is a bad person. Perhaps later on your spiritual journey you will reach a certain plateau in your spiritual evolution, when you are so strong and centered, that those same people will not bring you down. Then, you may even enjoy their company, or even help them in some way, without their presence affecting your truth. I have found the importance of allowing myself to be around all kinds of people ... those who are spiritually mature, those who are on the verge of discovering something awesome, and those who allow others to depict their life for them. The beauty of being around people who are different from you, is to allow yourself a chance to be challenged so that further growth can occur.

One of the most fundamental truths that I must express is that every person, no matter what their choices have been, was created from the Divine and is still a part of the Divine. This may seem like a far-fetched idea, but in my eyes, it is truth. The sooner you allow yourself to see the Divine in all people, the quicker you will allow yourself to be free. Freeing yourself frees others.

# CHAPTER 10

## Heaven Is Right in Front of You

*Both abundance and lack exist simultaneously in our lives, as parallel realities. It is always our conscious choice which secret garden we will tend... when we choose not to focus on what is missing from our lives but are grateful for the abundance that's present / love, health, family, friends, work, the joys of nature and personal pursuits that bring us pleasure / the wasteland of illusion falls away and we experience Heaven on earth.*

Sarah Ban Breathnach

The Inner Mind is still.

The Soul reflects the Most High.

The Spirit of man is God.

In the great calm of the All good,

I rest in peace and security.

My life is now reflecting the Perfect Whole.

I am Peace; I am calm
I am security and complete satisfaction
I am One with God.
I am filled with peace.

Ernest Holmes

The Divine Presence is readily available within each of our hearts as often as we are willing to allow it to come forth. An important part of our Presence is the actual illumination of our Divine hearts. There are many ways to get away from the pressures of life, and meditation and prayer are options we can choose to partake in as an important part of our joy as human beings. Our balance in life relies on our being in touch with That Which is True... and when our minds are quiet then only divinity can manifest in our entire being. Find what makes you calm; find what makes you see the world from a perspective of beauty. It may be meditation, yoga classes or prayer in moments of stillness. There is no wrong or right way to pray or to meditate. For me, I enjoy listening to music to center myself and to feel in balance. I also enjoy playing basketball, mowing the grass, and writing. Each of these activities are a way of taking myself into the present moment. If I am able to focus only on that which I am doing then I am living in the present moment and experiencing joy. The key is to find things that you love to do... you do not want prayer or meditation to be something that you have to do or that you do not look forward to doing. There is peace in meditation and prayer, and if you can find peace through activities, through stillness, or through other ways then that peace will reflect your heart.

When I was six years old, my parents were asleep when my father was woken by a knock at the door. Somehow, my mother didn't budge, but my father knew he had to go to the door. During the weeks and days before this very moment, my parents had been jobless, confused, and searching for an answer. So, my father, in the midst of trying to wake up, made it to the front door and opened it. Before him was his grandmother, who had passed away several years before.

Shocked, my father asked, "What are you doing here?"

And she replied, "I am here to tell you that everything is going to be okay."

My father hesitated and asked, "What do you mean?"

She said again, "I am here to tell you that everything is going to be okay." My great-grandmother then turned around and faded slowly as she walked away.

The next day, my father got an opportunity of work eight hours away from all that we knew, and we moved from Kentucky to Mississippi with nothing but faith and hope. Leaving our extended family behind, my older brother, my younger brother, my parents, and I took a leap of faith together. Today my father's business that he started nearly 20 years ago is thriving, growing, and has provided stability for my family in every way.

In a world that is demanding, confusing, and constantly asking for our best, it is easy to forget that everything will be okay because we are ONE. With the pressures that we put on our shoulders each and every day it is nice to be reminded to relax and just breathe. Along the way, my parents have taught me to trust my intuition, to go with my heart. Although some say that "following your heart" is clichéd, the truth of the matter is that when you follow your heart ... you are allowing the moment to take precedence.

When my parents decided to make the move to Mississippi, it was a testimony to trusting in what the universe was going to create for my family. My parents let go of the past, and with a future that was unknown, decided to live in the moment ... and the moment of consciousness revealed prosperity! My great-grandmother who came to my father that night expressed the importance of trusting what is ... and sometimes we need a reminder to ... guess what? Remain in the moment and trust all that is ... because it is what it is. In a life that comes and goes so quickly, take a moment to stop and smell the roses because if you don't, summer will end and fall always comes too fast.

We live in a society that tests our ability to appreciate what is currently in front of us. I have learned that the most prominent way to live is to allow the moment to be in my consciousness. If I am aware of who I am right now … not who I was … or who I might be … then I can discover every new desire that aligns with my purpose, and with every new discovery my light gets a little bit brighter. If my light is able to shine, not only am I experiencing freedom, but so are others who cross my path. My approach to life affects those around me, and if I can live in the moment, then I can love myself, and if I love myself then the Divine becomes clearer. No matter what you believe to be true about God, a Higher Power, Buddha, or life itself, living in the moment shows us that we all can experience a similar guidance of spirit by recognizing the divine part of who we are as individuals.

Take on the new outlook of finding what is perfect about you and not what is "imperfect" about you and celebrate life by focusing on what is front of you at this very moment. No matter what your situation or circumstance is, life is a beautiful opportunity to share splendor with others so that they may share theirs with you. The abundance of life is in our own hands ... all we have to trust in is, "that everything is going to be okay." Because, everything *is* really going to be okay! You are worthy of the joy of life, and so am I ... so, let's travel this journey together and make this a path of cleansing.

I believe that our time on this earth, in this universe, is to be enjoyed. If you are a teacher, an orthodontist, a geologist, or a coach ... and if you want to be a professor, a doctor, or a lawyer ... all in all, remember that our purpose is to love ourselves so that we can fully express our passions and creativity. I do know that my purpose in life is to love, and with that, all that I do is just another opportunity to touch a life, another chance to learn, and another moment to smile. In realizing our worth, we find the worth of others, and the worth of everything around us ... somehow, leading us back to what we first experienced as a child ... Love. Heaven is here, right now.

# CHAPTER 11

## Questions That Are Often Asked of Me

*How do you justify the suffering that children
in poorer parts of the world endure?*

I believe that we each live many lives and that our souls choose
what setting we will be born into. I believe that we come into
this world with particular lessons we would like to learn. It
will be our choices, in our current life, as human beings that
will determine if we learn these lessons, whatever they may
be. For me, I believe that a great lesson I am learning is to
have complete faith in the process of life and to allow it to
manifest that which comes from my heart, which is where
the essence of God resides. Because this is a lesson that I
am constantly faced with, I am learning to love on a greater

level, learning to live in higher consciousness, and to live my truth with immense passion. Through this, I am learning that heaven can be on earth if I allow it to be.

### *What about children who are born with cancer, severe disabilities, and other diseases?*

My answer to this question is very similar to that above. I believe that we choose the physical state that we will appear in for our life to learn specific lessons. I also think that people with diseases or people with severe disabilities are here to teach us great lessons about life. We so often forget about the simple joys that life offers us, and a lot of times we are reminded of these joys by someone else's example. A lesson that continually comes forth through people, for me, is the lesson to live in the moment, to appreciate the moment, and to fall in love with the moment.

### *Why is there so much violence in the world? Why would God let that happen?*

To some people there is often great mystery in violence. We often ask the question, why can't we all just get along? My answer to this question is simple: we all make our own choices. Violence occurs because as human beings we have free will, and unfortunately, some people choose to turn toward violence rather than to love. I do not believe that God/Spirit/Energy allows violence to happen to us ... in fact, I don't think God allows anything to happen without our first requesting it on some level. As part of God, we are involved in the continuing process of creating our reality and experiences—through our thoughts and choices. Thought patterns appear to create reality through the Law of Attraction. It appears that fear and thoughts of violence may attract violence, whereas love and thoughts of peace will attract their counterparts.

I believe that if I trust in complete faith that I will find a partner who is passionate, supportive and loving, then that person will find a way into my life. I believe that if I want a job with particular qualities, God will find a way to allow that to walk into my life. I believe that if we collectively know that peace is going to occur in our world, then major changes will be made and that we WILL evolve into that state of being. However, my friends, faith does not involve doubt, it does not involve hesitation ... faith is knowing what will be ... and it *will* be because you *know* it.

### Why do bad things happen to good people?

Again, we are the creators of our lives. We are the masters

of our perceptions. I consider myself a good person, but what is a "bad thing"? What if someone I love dies? Then, I might ask, what have I done to lose this person? I have done nothing … that is the process of life, that we may all live and that we may all die. We die according to our choices in life and according to the choices of others. We affect one another's paths and I do believe that all people are inherently and spiritually good and pure. I think also that there are not people who are inherently "bad."

I also believe that when I am in pain, or when something tough happens that I must move past, I am wiser when I make it through, that I am stronger, and that I am able to love even more deeply. All that we encounter in our own worlds are situations that we can either run away from or deal with. If you choose to deal with any situation you encounter, then your progression as a loving being will consistently bring you to a place of greater knowing, of greater understanding, and to a greater passion for life as it is. If we choose to run away from a particular situation, then it will result in growth ultimately; however, the choice is more in relation to how you choose to deal with an event. As we walk on our own journeys, our own paths, we find tough circumstances; but, it is our choice how we will continue to move through those circumstances.

An awareness and understanding of the true nature of things will probably smooth your ride, and more readily enable you to respond with Love.

### What happens to us when we die?
### Isn't heaven a place we go after our physical life is over?

Great question! I believe that heaven is here. I believe that we are amidst heaven in our everyday life … and that we create our heaven based on our beliefs, actions, and choices. My hope is that this book demonstrates to you that it is possible to perceive heaven right here and now … that each moment can be looked upon as something beautiful and meaningful. I never said that there will never be tough moments, but I do believe that we have all we need to move through those tough moments and to come out as people who have progressed, grown, and can inspire others to do the same. Heaven is in *this moment*.

When we die, I believe our spirit lifts from our body back into a state of peace and it makes its choice as to where it will move to. I believe that we are in the constant presence of God, whether we have died or whether we are living on this earth, and that we are constantly evolving – becoming ONE as a whole by recognizing we are all a part of the same essence … the essence of LOVE.

### *Does hell exist?*

Every one of us has a different idea of what hell is. I believe that hell is created in our minds, and that we can choose to live in hell on earth. I believe that when we are consistently choosing to live in pain and choosing not to live in Love, that we create our own hell on this earth. Just as you can create heaven on earth, I do believe that you can create hell based on your choices.

### *Is there a devil?*

I believe that "the devil" resides in our minds. If we use the definition of what the devil is, the Merriam-Webster definition says, "chief spirit of evil and adversary of God"—then we find that the devil can in fact be a product of our minds. If my mind is constantly in fear of what might happen, then I may just create what my mind is asking for. For example, if I am always afraid that I will never get that perfect job, then more than likely, I will never get that perfect job. Therefore, I am creating a lack of Love in my life, a lack of faith, which makes my mind "an adversary of God" (of Love).

### *Where does "evil" come from?*

As I have said before, I believe that we as a human race

131

contribute to the creation of "evil". If everyone is good and pure, you may ask, then how is there evil in the world? I am using the word "evil" as an expression of our choices; that we may choose to act in a way that causes pain to ourselves or to others. I do not believe that God/Spirit/Love creates evil, or creates pain, in our lives to challenge us... I believe that we contribute to bringing pain and disharmony into the world, like we can contribute to bringing peace and joy to the world! That puts a lot of responsibility on our shoulders, does it not? Yes, of course it does, because we are always looking for others to blame when our egos are tested. But, yes, I do believe that we contribute to the creation of pain or suffering, when we are choosing to not live in Love.

### Is there such a thing as reincarnation?

I believe in reincarnation. I believe that I have lived before, and that I have lived many, many times. I believe that I have evolved into who I am today and that I will continue to evolve into a more loving and more trusting being. I think our spirits are the true essence of what the universe is made of and that it is all God/Love/Spirit—that we are all ONE. I believe that we are evolving into a loving space and into a space that most consider to be heaven—where we can all live in peace.

I think that we are connected to specific souls more strongly than others, but that we are all connected. I believe our connectedness to specific people is based on our relationships from past lives and that we are continually moving toward ultimate love with those relationships. Have you ever met someone and thought you had met that person before, but never really had? Why do you think that was? There is a beautiful and all-encompassing Omnipresence out there and we have a choice whether to acknowledge It and work with It, or to continue to live with no progression, no movement toward greatness.

### What is the purpose of it all?

To evolve into Love. When are we going to stop evolving? I believe we will stop evolving when we are all willing to live in Love. For now, it is the challenge of finding and following our own purpose that is before us. What is your purpose? I wish I could tell you ... I do not know what your passions are; I do not know what your heart is asking of you—I only know that you are to listen to your heart, that you are to follow the path that is true for you, and that you are to create your heaven on this earth. If we live in heaven as individuals, then people around us will want to find their heaven as well. This is the difference in the world that we can make as individuals and it comes through how we choose to live our own lives. You are only responsible for your Truth…and there is a powerful, powerful message that we each send to those who are in our lives by living in Love, by living in our Truth. We are all fully capable and are equipped for any circumstance we are presented with—and yes, we are fully capable of happiness!

# Helpful Reading

Bach, Richard (1977) *Illusions.* Creature Enterprises, Inc.

Chopra, Deepak (1994) *The Seven Spiritual Laws of Success.*
San Rafael, CA: Amber-Allen Publishing, Inc.

Chopra, Deepak (2006) *Power, Freedom, and Grace.* San Rafael,
CA: Amber-Allen Publishing, Inc.

Coelho, Paulo (2006) *The Alchemist.* New York, NY:
HarperCollins Publishers.

Frankl, Viktor (1959) *Man's Search for Meaning.* Beacon, MA:
Beacon Press.

Frankl, Viktor (2000) *Man's Search for Ultimate Meaning.*
Perseus Publishing.

Gibran, Kahlil (1923) *The Prophet.* Alfred A. Knoff, Inc.

King, Joan (2008) *Cellular Wisdom for Women.* Fort Collins,
CO: Word Keepers, Inc.

Millman, Dan (2006) *Way of the Peaceful Warrior.* Novato,
Canada: New World Library.

Quinn, Gary (2005) *Living in the Spiritual Zone.* Hodder
Mobius.

Redfield, James (1993) *The Celestine Prophecy.* New York, NY:
Warner Books, Inc.

Ruiz, Don Miguel (2000) *The Four Agreements*. San Rafael,
    CA: Amber-Allen Publishing, Inc.

Ruiz, Don Miguel (2004) *The Voice of Knowledge*. San Rafael, CA:
    Amber-Allen Publishing, Inc.

Teilhard de Chardin, Pierre (2000) *Building the Earth*.
    Dimension Books.

Tolle, Eckhart (1999) *The Power of Now*. Novato, Canada:
    New World Library.

Tolle, Eckhart (2007) *A New Earth*. Novato, Canada: New
    World Library.

Vanzant, Iyanla (1999) *Yesterday I Cried*. Simon and Schuster, Inc.

Zukav, Gary (1989) *The Seat of the Soul*. New York, NY:
    Fireside.

*Celebrating Holi—the author and Atal Behari Vajpayee*

# Confessions of a Swadeshi Reformer

# Confessions of a Swadeshi Reformer

## My Years as Finance Minister

*YASHWANT SINHA*

**PENGUIN**
**VIKING**

VIKING
Published by the Penguin Group
Penguin Books India Pvt. Ltd, 11 Community Centre, Panchsheel Park,
New Delhi 110 017, India
Penguin Group (USA) Inc., 375 Hudson Street, New York, New York 10014, USA
Penguin Group (Canada), 90 Eglinton Avenue East, Suite 700, Toronto,
Ontario, M4P 2Y3, Canada (a division of Pearson Penguin Canada Inc.)
Penguin Books Ltd, 80 Strand, London WC2R 0RL, England
Penguin Ireland, 25 St Stephen's Green, Dublin 2, Ireland
(a division of Penguin Books Ltd)
Penguin Group (Australia), 250 Camberwell Road, Camberwell,
Victoria 3124, Australia (a division of Pearson Australia Group Pty Ltd)
Penguin Group (NZ), 67 Apollo Drive, Rosedale, North Shore 0632,
New Zealand (a division of Pearson New Zealand Ltd)
Penguin Group (South Africa) (Pty) Ltd, 24 Sturdee Avenue, Rosebank,
Johannesburg 2196, South Africa

Penguin Books Ltd, Registered Offices: 80 Strand, London WC2R 0RL, England


First published in Viking by Penguin Books India 2007

Copyright © Yashwant Sinha 2007

Photographs courtesy of the author

All rights reserved

10 9 8 7 6 5 4 3 2 1

The views and opinions expressed in this book are the author's own and the facts are as
reported by him which have been verified to the extent possible and the publishers are not in
any way liable for the same.

ISBN-13: 978-0-67099-952-1      ISBN-10: 0-67099-952-0

Typeset in *Sabon Roman* by SÜRYA, New Delhi
Printed at Gopsons Papers Ltd, Noida